I am Carolina

celebrating the nature of the Carolinas

poems by

Philip Comfort

Finishing Line Press
Georgetown, Kentucky

I am Carolina

Celebrating the Nature of the Carolinas

ACKNOWLEDGMENTS

Some of the poems appeared before in *Wings* and *Seascapes* (both published by
Finishing Line Press)

Publisher: Leah Maines

Editor: Christen Kincaid

Author Photo: Peter Comfort

Cover Design: Elizabeth Maines McCleavy

Printed in the USA on acid-free paper.
Order online: www.finishinglinepress.com
        also available on amazon.com

Author inquiries and mail orders:
Finishing Line Press
P. O. Box 1626
Georgetown, Kentucky 40324
U. S. A.

Table of Contents

I am Carolina
Celebrating the Nature of the Carolinas

These poems celebrate the life of seas, coastal creatures, coastal life, rivers, savannahs, woodlands, mountains, and nature of the Carolinas. It begins with the Northern Outer Banks of North Carolina, moves inland to the mountains and then goes back to the coast of North Carolina, continues down the coast to the furthest southern tip of South Carolina. On the journey down the South Carolina coast I go inland to the Francis Marion Woods and the Ace Basin for a while and then return to the coast. There are more poems in the Pawleys Island area than the other coastal places because that is my hometown. Pawleys Island is a three-mile island in South Carolina, surrounded by a wide creek running through a marsh. All of coastal Carolina, open to the ocean and the heavens, has inspired spiritual meditations and incantations. These coastal lands and beaches have provided me with liberation of spirit, incantations, and imaginations. I had the experiences and observations described in these poems, but I took some poetic license to place them in various locations.

The Australian aborigines read their landscape as a manuscript communicating a divine message. I read the Carolina seascape and landscape as communications from God. I read the sea by surfing it and walking along it, and I read the landscape by hiking or kayaking through it. Thousands of years before the aborigines and thereafter humans have contacted and communicated with the spirit world through nature. The 36,000 year old cave drawings in the Chauvet Cave of France reveal that humans were seeking contact with spirits though nature. This search has continued throughout human history, and I have participated in it. God is Spirit, and this Spirit is found in waves, wind, and coastal lands—for God is in all and through all. In the poems I commune with Spirit God, who reveals himself to me through nature. What I witnessed in nature was inspiring, an inspiration which continued on in the writing (I hope)—God being present in the natural event and in the writing event. In some poems I commune with Spirit God by reaching out to him as in prayer or praise.

music of the sea

music maker, soul-waker,
your fingers cross the ivory,
coast the keys like seabirds
over waves, taking melodies
to fantastic exotic lands—
your music assumes limbs
your tunes incarnate wings
that fly me places livelier
than dreams and poems

not claiming space, passing through
odiferous perfume, a lingering aura.
not overpowering, sweet companion,
this is what I love about you.

you are music that moves toward
my face and touches me deeply—
your expressions my eyes applaud
and my heart rises in ovation

for Georgia, my beloved wife

Opening Prayer

God, make me a manuscript
the wild animal
stretch, dry, gloss
take the slim inkhorn
filled with black charcoal
dried to crust
moisten the split reed
dip stylus into my thoughts
before they wing off

Prologue Poem
I am Carolina

I am rollinggreen meadows, tan savannahs,
liveOaks drapped with SpanishMoss
oldAsGod, riceplantations with songs of slaves
still lingering in the damp sunsoaked air.
I am Ace Basin—marsh swamp meanderingRivers
snakingstreams meanderingcreeks sandyislands
ocean-surroundedspits slimcays curvedcapes
coasts lining the livingblue-greenocean—
Iam alive with me, alive with zoe,
alive with spiritWindGod and ghosts
who never wanted to leave this birthOfEarth—
this breathOfSseabirdsAlligatorsDolphinsDogs
huntingLife, catchingGod, livingInlife's death
as both the same with different names.
Iam the Carolinas soaked with water
from springRains, runningStreams,
lowlandCreeks, oceanWavesandMist,
clouds as longasgods from sunrise to sunset
light, dark, and ark for creatures
millenniaGoneandmillenniaMore—
I am homeland to the first Americans
habitat of Cherokee, Wacammaw, and Edisto
alive with mana, spiritCreatures, livingSprites—
Iam alive, and Iam life.
I can't be snared or sepulchred
IamWavesFetchFrothFoamPelicanStorkGullLoon
Iam seaSpillreefBreakgullSplashrockCrash
tidePushmoonPullfishFlushbirdSwarmwindDraft
Iam waterOuzel slippingFall earthShifting
movingMeadows sinkingFurrows
Iam divinescent flowerooze sundrink
that brokenopen essence that flick that kick
that slightest touch of monarchlegs
on branchbend in floweryawn
Iam caw crawl fishspurt grainsprout
bobcatBounding pumaSleekness forestRain

seapeeling earthbreaking sunsoaking lifescent
that earthturned wiff eyeglint joyburstAftersadness
sigh touch of invisibleQuick
      I Spiritmove intoEveryLivingThingIam
I dewdescend on spiders' webs
the diamond crystals in translucentSun
I chamelion green lizardbacks to brown
lighten murkiness Let darkness cloud
      I do not come to reason or defend
but transform U g LY to thin and flat to ROUND
ubiquitous, I cannot flee—nor you me
IamFalconflightWindhold
Iam hermit crab's search for conch
man's dream other planets are not parched
Iam spiritBreathpneumaAir
IamRushFountainWingsMotion
no cistern can hold me square
      I MoveMentoGladness
console bereft in their despairsadness
by unexpected magnoliaBloom
the breaking of exoticScent
heaven's jar unscrewed and poured
      whatever has being has being in me
can't you see me in a thousand figures?
lovely limbs, uncommon faces
signatured, distinct, unscrolled
each takes its shape from within
and shouts to the glories, IAm
      I will never be endangered though hunted
by all religions who haven't figured
Iam tideSurge windDrop treeFall
mushroomSproutspriggedLeaftreeRot
s t r e a k e d sunset blackcatdarkness
Iam tidechange sucked back over smooth stones
clacking in liquid s w o o s h and waveSurge
      can't you see Iam Carolina spirit?
all that ISaliveISalive with me

the peaTendril reaching for staked post
the redFox chasing bald pink sun
the mother milking twins with double tits
I feed all—Iam nutrient never spent
I sustain flesh with spirit—they are lent
until I take them back again.
this is not cruel or fluke or fair
this is what is and what is meant
                nothing can diminish me
as the tall rice-stalks wave in the wind
don't think they have no thought for me—
freshly mown, smell its sweetSacrifice
oo are each of the trillion deaths to me
the squishedAnts scream and hooked fish
(their end is no less human)
                I cannotstop or backlook on what I was
for Iam vineblood humanserum spit and sperm
sap of Rinsoaked sweetcane
chickorycluster poking blue
through speckledgray rockcrack
Iam rushingstream oceancurrent
d o l p h i n g l i d e a n d p l u n g e
seahawk s w o o p ClawandTongue
fishwriggle flash and fetch
                I journey my biography
for Iam as Iwas and willbe as Iam
I cannot be FetteredForgotten
Iam aftermilennia afterHaveComeandGone
and the earth has no morsels left to give
Iam a million mouths at once
underOnAbove the scalloped masses
a sea of leaves revealing this:
the floweringWave is sure as my lips
for Iam always and always is
and I am Carolina

Northern Outer Banks, North Carolina

Scanning the Wet Wild Waves

my ears see before my eyes
as I mount a knoll in North Carolina
        wet wild wind in my face
I scan long lines of distant waves undulating toward shore
in sets of four or five like fingers of some invisible hand
moving sideways just beneath the water's blue surface
        silent as darkness where nothing has voice.
I notice the fingers gradually knuckling up into bowed shapes
        while hearing closer waves drumming their end;
suddenly the fingers transfigure into liquid leviathans
        bellowing, hissing, moaning, roaring,
as the waves mount up into evanescent griffins—
stallions charging with spindrift manes, lurching behemoths
        crashing outer reefs, spewing white-high plumes
        I have no speech! as I gape
at their mammoth faces breaking open, peeling, closing,
throwing down their vicious power on the rocks
like snowy leopards running in from the chase—
the kill, the spill of bestial music:
        poured out primordial booms accompanied by
        the fastest snare rolls I've ever heard—
        percussion peeking wild then thinning smooth
        like sizzler cymbals, morocco shakers,
        brush strokes on taut antelope skin
        played by some invisible hands.

Walking the Beach and Thinking Pangaea

As I walk the sea on a northern spit of land
    I think of a time before continents drifted apart—
        what phenomena! only one landmass called Pangaea
    an island surrounded by mighty Panthalassa—
the Carolinas had an ancient terrestrial border
    before they were exposed to the moving ocean waters.
        I wonder what mammals roamed the ancient shores
    and what humans were the first to wade and plunge deep
in the aqua and white waves breaking on the beach—
    this is all beyond my imagination and mind's reach.
        fifteen thousand years ago, according to paleontologists,
    the first Americans wandered the mountains and coasts
hunting for wild food on high and in the plunging surf—
    but—think of it!—it's not until our own modern times
        that anyone paddled a surfboard down the peeling line
    and rode a wave billowing, cascading, breaking sublime—
I am one of those who visits the ocean not for fish
    but to hunt waves that rise and roll to the beach,
        enjoying the aqua flow and water's push and rush—
    making me think some ancient natives also rode the line
in boats carved out of thick, tall southern pines
so I and they, like continents, are only separated by time

Walking the Beach and Thinking of the First Carolinian

as I walk the beach
I imagine the first
Carolinian wet with spirit,
warmed by sun and blood,
strolling under skies—
oceans of it, stars in it,
white waves of it.
He admired the clouds
between him and there—
better for sunrise,
sweeter for sunset,
for gazing, for wondering,
for listening to waves
shaping beaches,
to rain spawning rivers,
to spirit swirling winds
between waves and thoughts.
He roved shores wondering
why he had come to this,
figuring wave rush, crush,
splash, lunge pushed him
from sea to sand,
feeling that some greater
force had breathed
him into being, had moved
him from wish to flesh,
had incarnated some
unspoken primal quest.
He desired migration
in the glistening waves
in the going somewhere
beyond darkening horizons,
for he was island
and all his desires sea.

Watching Waves Curling the Carolinas

unmanned ocean curls the Carolinas
      rides its lovers out to sea
and hurls them back again
      on roaring aqua surf.
the raw sacred motion
      of savage holy union
primes procreation seen—
      sea gives birth to surf and sands
ocean erupts naked islands
      sprouting glistening palms
and waterfalls running
      to wet their wild nativity.
its mystic sway juices Islanders like me
      with rains that come and leave

Discovering a Drum Circle

I by luck come across a drum circle—
congas conk, cowbells clang, cymbals ting,
    tap tap tap, stroke stroke stroke
bongos ping, rimshot rips, tomtoms flare
    bang bang bang, blam blam blam
tablas thud, bassdrum booms, tamberines chink
    boom boom boom, click click click
punctuated by breaking surf: crash, surge, sizzle.
    the circle feels the primal pulse
    percuss, percuss in syncopated thrust
as if it were a cylinder for the primeval voice—
    bass booms depths (throbbing hearts)
    congas climb into spirits that prance
        animal-like, howl and hoot, jump and shout
click tongue and throat—as jungle and ocean mingle
in oval primeval rushing mix of sound all around
    paradiddle paradiddle, flamcue flamcue
        rrrrrrrrrrrrrrrooooooooooooooollllllllllllllllllllll
ring ring ring crash; ping ping ping splash
slam tap slam tap slam tap. plash plash plash
five-stroke roll, seven-stroke roll, click click click
quick on every drum with flailing sticks and hands
    connecting each drummer to the vibe of being
    less than a beat away from Eden

Kitty Hawk, Outer Banks, North Carolina

Caught in Glory

these waves have come from where I've never been
    I know them only in their end
        these bendingTumblers, sleekDivers, plungingHeaders
        who spirit the *skene* one majestic minute
    then just as quickly ghost away.
what puissance primedPumpedPushed them
    into performance is never told by their faces
    which surfers glide across leaving impermanent traces
of having caught them in their glory

Under a Slow Sky

slow sky awakes over a surging ocean
      mauve clouds crawl along the horizon
      the earth gives birth to glowing sun
      as high tide swells and swallows beach—
I'm being eaten by the divine
      gulped down by the oracle of God—
      will I have anything to sing?
my dog barks at the beachcombers
they answer with percussive breaks
      thumping, drumming, crashing, sizzling
I'm surrounded by the sound of Spirit
alive with Christ becoming crests
I drink Jesus' Spirit and live like sun
      winging to the next long horizon

Breathing with the Sea

Absorbing sunbreak and moonfall longer than bones,
      earth's eyeball, over half the globe,
looks upward, not at us, peering at galaxies of God,
      while this turf has sucked the best and mean
and is the heavier for having taken down.

Not the ocean that survives with soul,
      it has a way of breathing.
Nothing I can say could make it swell—
      dwarfed by its majesty I am dumb
but not deaf—the seawinds are my prophets.

Empires peak and crash—Babylon, Greece, Rome,
England, and other proud predicted powers—
      but the sea sees none of them,
nor does the seawinged seahawk hovering wind,
      scanning waves, eyes fixed on ocean
until catching a phosphorescent flash of bluefish
      falls quick as light with open talons.

They will be this again and again
      the sea the sun the hawk the wind
long after everything human into humus has fallen.

Sensing the Moving of God

He moves between the breaking seas
    in dark mystery.

Pelicans wing along the peeling waves.

The eyes of God, the face of man—
    you are not quite one of us.

The disk drops darkness and it is cold.

He makes eternity palpable, almost
    attainable. Almost.

The clouds eat sunset and are gone.

He lingers somewhere near the broken
    soul and quiet breath.

Seagulls and pelicans warm winter waters.

Some say he appears as dolphin. As savior
    of the drowning.

Dogs chase waves. Men chase dogs and days.

Too fast. Too swift the kick from here to there.
    But he makes it.

Kill Devil Hills, Outer Banks, North Carolina

Surfing the Swelling Sea

the Outer Banks, with stronglong beaches
    and offshore breezes on swellingSea
azure, clear, and primed, a soulsurfer's dream
    (can't believe it!) that you gave me
longStrongRides on pristine waves—
    (how sweet!) the shape, the peak, the feel
of dropping in before the peelingBreak
    of sliding along a headhighcrest,
a mounting moving liquid face,
    of tucking under the windwhipped curl
as it began to bend (and I thought would fall),
    but the wall held stiff by offshore gust
as I thrust into its hallowedness
    and entered a blessed sphere
where there's nothing but wind-and-sea,
    and I, an awed intruder (o spirit!),
who then slid out into foamingfroth
    where a rainbowSpray appeared
as miraculous as the wave (I caught it!)

Scanning the Outside Breakers

outside past poundingbreakers
a crowd of surfers sit deep, scan west,
squinting at sun dropping into Albemarle Sound
like a wafer dipped in wine

I watch them bobbing up and down
in swelling mounds, their longboards
arching up like the sanddunes
behind them catchingfallingRays

while they all wait, passing waves
lillyUp, shovelDown, and break
into hundreds of thundered shreds—
and then they see, as I see, a swell
swallowing horizon, speeding their way

one surfer paddlesDeep into the almighty
quick drops, heart stops, crouching
at the feet of the immanent Mover
who allows one epiphanic ride
down an uncertain line of liquidPower
until it frothsHissesThinsHushes

Catching a Peeling Break

I catch breath, dive underneath summersaulting break,
       surface, bite another waveMountReelPeel:
out of eternal circular flatness it mounds up
       in multiple moving faces, walls up, glistens diaphanous,
bends fistulous, breaksBucklesFalls in percussive rushes.

Looking back I see tumbled sun burst white, turn thin light,
       sizzle out, as each wave—quicklife—is sucked back to sea.

When ocean reveals itself in flash of opened face,
       the cast becomes a voice pitched as apocalypse—
a voice I first heard when the ocean began
       hurling revelations so potent I was felled to my knees,
forced to measure my liquesence, the compass of my fetch.

Yet it's so hard to say the mystery I've heard, for as quick
       as it's revealed, the sea scrolls itself into a roll I can't read.

Whenever I hear clouds coming and horses running on water,
       I paddle into a herd of waves and let one after another pass
until there's one that bends its neckAndgallops me to shore.
       I know that's why I return again and again like waves—
I have hopes of unraveling lips as I catch a peeling break.

Surfing a Long Right

a long right
a steep right
a hollow right
a memorable right
never interrupted by fall
a long right
a good right
a smooth right
an eternal right
that is what I look for
in the crooked
most of the time
I can't find it
but once in a while it's there
peaceful like uncalculated air
just floating between hemispheres
waiting for me to catch it
hanging there to fetch it
and when I get it, it gets me
there is nothing as good
nothing as free
not anyone has hallowed out
such a sacred groove
this is not to say I'm good
only occasionally lucky

Listening to Ocean Oracle

he mornings deathdark shadows
        dips day into darkest night
buckets oceans of heavy water
        sprinkles earth with precious rains
carves mountains, stirs winds,
        reveals his thoughts to quiet beings

after one sun falls into the ocean
        the night sun rises heaven's queen
with an entourage of circled stars
        who make the heaven's music—
yes, there's a singing in heaping stars
        (spoon mouthfuls of cymbals, drink timbrels!)

divine drones oscillate in orbits
        percussing rhythmic waves on our drums
(tune them beyond our sphere);
        though most have drowned the oracles
there are those who swim watery worlds
        who've always sung pelagic poems

I paddle out, lay prone on the flat sea
        (ear to the deep) in quiet uncertainty
await the epiphany emerging quick
        in those who pierce the membrane,
spit darkness, squeal light, dive back
        (don't be dumb, catch the sight)

Lost in Gray

the cape is grayAsSeals
gray withMist withSea withRain
with colorless clapboard cottages
facing the ocean spotted with trawlers
trailed by hungry gray herons
       the only thing I saw that wasn't gray
was a red fox c h a s i n g a white rabbit—
all else is lostInGrayness
as sky meltsIntoRainIntoSea

Nags Head, Outer Banks, North Carolina

If I Could Be Wind of Ocean

when Jesus walked on the Sea of Galilee
he did so as wind, as spirit, as free
the terrified disciples saw him as a phantom—
a ghost through miraculous transfiguration.
      Peter couldn't believe this transformation,
so he fell into the sea like anyone would
who is composed of flesh and blood.

I'd love to be transfigured and translucent
so I could be wind of ocean—
      for now, I limp along Nags Head beach
and realize this is all out of reach
but one day I will falcon-fly, pelican-dive
      dolphin-porpoise, wind-phantom on the ocean

seven Spirits search the earth
for those who know what moves this orb—
it is wind, it is spirit, it is ocean, it is breath

Amazed by Big Wave Surfers

driven by winter storms in the north Atlantic Ocean
        humongousWaves leapUp and form as half moons
rising to twenty feet tall off the Outer Banks coast
        which are ridden by big-wave East Coast surfers—
the waves lurchForward twenty seconds apart
        they are thickandhuge, like white bulldozers,
too large for any surfer to paddle against—
        some stoked surfers get rides on jet-skis
up and over and beyond the massive breakers
        where they form just before their rising—
they hitch a ride on a ski-tow that propels them
        into the biggest surge on the Carolinas
then they surf down the face in a perfect line
        getting a rush of wave and rush of blood
joining a moment of the creationOfGod

across the Atlantic ocean directly to the east
        the same sea swell surges, makingWavesHeave,
rising at their apex to a HundredFeetTALL
        near the beach Praia do Norte in Nazare, Portugal.
standing high on the platform of a lighthouse
        spectators have the most amazing place on earth
to watch surfers ride the biggestLiquidMammoths—
        how their hearts must beat as surfers jump to their feet
and glide in nearFree-fall down a huge sheet
        of moving blue wave, white-waterCascadingBehind,
cruising down and to the right trying to find
        the route that will save them from the fall
of a crushingCrashingWall that could cause their spill—
        their demise could come quick in the ocean's breath
but God is so near when a soul's close to death

Catching the Fetch

       when a groundswell r o l l s i n, bellowing,
billowingCurlingTrimmingFeathering
       percussing arpeggio across this archipelago
the sea becomes my kithara and muse.
       I immerse myself to fetch that voice
I first heard between cadence and crash—
       the voice that spills from lips of waves
in the timbre of variegated aeolian peaks
       crestingToCrescendo fallingInMoreno;
somewhere in there between the breaks
       I hear the oracle that makes life sense
seagullCaw, seahawkSilentGlide, pelicanDive
       into an ocean more majestic than awe.
rise. wind. wave. spirit. verve. I call
       God who is coming God who has come,
the end is nothing more than what has been:
       wind singing sea, sea surging bends and breaks—
in l o n g s t r o n g cascades waves musicate

Rodanthe, Outer Banks, North Carolina

Invoking an Epiphany of Wind on Sea

the ocean sound is round. no separate gull of ocean.
　　　　no wave of its own unfolding. up and down the coast
I'd been invoking an epiphany of wind on sea.

　　　　a gaggle of waves, whitetopped, lining up, and pearling.
paddling till our arms ached, backs tightened, legs cramped
　　　　eyes squinting in sunbursts through colorshapes running

thickly, ghosting water, making all the white to grave rise.
　　　　froth, hoot, holler. Waves! who knows of tomorrow—
they may thin in west winds. they may calm halcyon at dusk.

　　　　but this day is goodGodcreated and I am graced to take these breaks.
the paddle. push. the jump. thrust. the weave. cut. the curve. slice.
　　　　the ride. glide　down long glacis, silent before crush, thick and sweet

as the boardturn swish, I and wave. wave and I in one rush
　　　　of naturalness. of no telling of the sea from me, as I charge its break
and wake and am thrust into sudden sacred hollowness

　　　　and come out flushed. flashed. having grasped the surge of, the pulse of
the primal ocean winging wet wild flinging soaked piles
　　　　of mounting moving waters making breaking taking me along and down.

Remembering my Dogangel

living on water and air and my love
I thought you'd make it to the warm days—
how you craved the sun as your body thinned
you still flared your nostrils to the wind
but couldn't chase. There was no more prance
left in you, though you wanted to please

the last good day together we shared the beach
and winter sun with two familiar dolphins
no more than a paddle away. They lit the ocean,
leaped, flipped, danced, dallied, played.
I know, Charlie, I know how you wanted to join—
you waded the frigid surf but couldn't swim.

the last grim days dragged slow as January
and I spoke nothing significant and couldn't change
the end, as we watched one cold sunset after another
die and I clung to keep the spirit of us alive
but I couldn't keep you from going to ghost—
I read it in your desperately sweet brown eyes.

the moment you left I went weeping to the drenched sea
I passed some children throwing bread and laughing
as a swarm of cawing seagulls circled overhead.
then they shouted with delight into the cold mist:
"look, dolphins!" and I saw the twins streaming silver,
sea's angels, as sure of where they were headed as eternity

remembering the day a glorious soul of a golden retriever
named Charlie left this earth and went to the next life

Waves, Outer Banks, North Carolina

Riding Slowforming Rollers

a dreamed-of morning
for riding slowforming rollers
for taking sleek quick runs
                    and soft salt falls
for diving into waves
                    as if I were seagull

my only companions—looping dolphins and languid sun—
didn't scan how board/feet/wave/run
but it doesn't matter for they know no wave ever lasts

and I don't mind it passing
            like the last best set
for another is bound to form on my horizon

Watching a Surfer

jumps flash dash tropical dark
                    quick thick glory breaking
dolphins splurge spin
                    dive plash
pelicans
fall
from
sky
like
rain
while southwest spirit lifts waves
sustains
a surfer
          slicing sideways
                    down steepsleek wall
of white chasinghimlikeavalanche
weaves in and out
               of furious surf
mounts up—brute stallion—takes off
cuts spins swirls
                  landing in trough
                    of sweet smooth sunned froth

Experiencing Ocean Gloam

dusk glows with a fiercer light than dawn
        it is the fantastic leaving of souls
it is the glory going, then gone
        as when cathedral candles are snuffed
        and smell strange in a dark room

first faint above thin pink wisps
        the moon ascending heavy surf now faces
straight across a spit of swaying seaoats
        the sunBuryingItselfIntoEarth
        and b l o o d y i n g the western scape of Waves

the crescent star has the glory of its fallen twin
        and lights the last two surfers taking turns
mountingAndDescending windwhippedPeaks
        until they t i r e and r e t r e a t to sand
where nocturnal glow claims dominion
        as it rises hIGHER on seesaw's end
        tilting upWard on seagull's wing

Braving Beastly Waves

hoping seafarer's luck, I brave the cold waves
        paddling out. hard. trounced.
                bounced back and pummeled.
before I know it the wave like some leviathan
        picksMeUp in its talons and throwsMeDown.
                I tumble in heavy water, not knowing
which way is up or down—I am about to drown
        in deep watery darkness strongerThanHades.
                my breath goes out of me and I suck in sea
I kick to the surface and vomit violently—
        all the while gasping for air in between heaves.
                I struggle to get back on my surfboard,
see a small break in between sets
        and ride it in all the way to Waves' beach,
                cursing, praying, thanking God that
though I just about died I actually got a ride.
        and so I paddle out again against the rush
                thinking this will be my death!

Joining in Seaside Soccer

as the sun and sea surge and splash
      men kick the soccer ball on the sandpacked beach—
back and forth their laughter lights the game
      as pass after pass thuds to shots between the posts,
some that are stopped and some that are goals
      but since no one keeps score, it doesn't matter.
what counts is fun for men who haven't lost what's young—
      on and on they play, making labored runs and passes,
everyone on offense and everyone on defense:
      "good ball" one shouts; "get back" another yells;
"goalosso" is praise raised from both sides of the shells.

there's something about the touch and roll of a soccer ball
      that never gets old—a flick of a kick renews!
how sweet the ball's flight, like seagulls on the wing,
      when it takes off and lands near a teammate's foot.
how cool the quick give-and-go, the one-timer,
      the deft header, the nut-megger, the shot on goal.
if the muscles didn't ache and lungs gasp for air,
      the ball could keep moving as long as day.
but even though the game must come to an end
      and the beachside be emptied of all that fun,
the ocean keeps kicking up foam, making run after run

Avon, Outer Banks, North Carolina

Watching Tow-in Surfers

the ancient Hawaiians called it *lele wa'a* (canoe leaping):
    seven men thrust a big canoe into the ocean
        and six paddlers got up enough speed to catch a ground swell
    while the seventh man, holding his board, leaped off the boat
onto a big wave and got a gorgeously l o n g l i q u i d r i d e

modern watermen call it tow-in surfing:
    a jet skier towing a surfer speeds breakneck
        into a wave as its movingMountingSurgingHigh
    and thrusts a foot-strapped surfer into the peak
of a twenty-footer or bigger—the taller, the thicker

in winter at Maui these waves get even larger—
    the few watermen who charge into these waves
        keep the Hawaiian spirit alive by chanting to the wind,
    channeling Akua-God and tuning their bodies, spirits, and minds
to the cycles and rhythms of the swells in the Kona and Trades

the night before they surf Jaws, they listen to pounding breaks
    and their pounding hearts; in the morning when they rise
        they stand on shore and feel the ground tremble underfoot
    as they watch the open ocean swell reach a shallow reef
and leap into a beauty of a beast they will dare to ride

in the winter season in the Outer Banks
    wild waves rise as high as the Frisco Pier near Avon—
        into which a jet skier carries the surfer to the break
    into treetop surf they could never paddle against
but hope they can ride to shore in horrificWind

some will wipe out in gnarly waves that sound
    and look as big as riverfalls—when the lip crashes
        on a surfer's head and sucks his body over the top
    and megatons of ocean pound concussive
pushing his body to darkDepths never been before

others will get the ride of their lives
    when in one momentous movement all the water
        gets sucked up the face (like at Pipeline)
    and it sets up perfectly: a s l o w, GIGANTIC barrel
so powerfully dangerous, so beautifully magnificent—

surfing the biggest movingMountain on this ocean planet
    is an adrenaline rush like no other granted, an incredible release,
        a freedom to be one (for one moment) with the living Creator
    as the surfer weaves his way down the mammoth face
and is graced with a momentOutOf Eternity

Riding the Wave

the sea surges in liquid peaks of cloud breaks
and crashes of white thunder in swift plunder
terribleness turning quickly serene—spilling on sandbars
into aqua green and translucent marine,
out of which another RISES with palmetto-high peaks,
blessed with supernatural mana SurfandSun—
making me wonder if Hebrews were the only chosen
and if paradise was ever lost at all

Buxton, Outer Banks, North Carolina

I Drink Sundawn Sea

sea and sky melt into each other's lines
      like quicksilver, mercurial, sleeksmooth
in glistening grays slipping cool over the horizon
      a comfortable dark, serene and unoppressive
over the wingSpreadglide of egrets
      and rolled waves bumping up like dolphinbacks
in the unscrolled moist oceanmorning mist
      settles in like pelican flock
hovering landing floating bobbing biding
      in the graywash, capecodish wetness
argent at surf's break, otherwise as solemn
      and silent as the surfers' wake at Buxton

I drink sundawn sea, mouth it moist,
      smell lightyears bouncing off the breaks
(supernovae breaking speed)
      mingled with fishswim old as God-thought
young as spindrift windkicked—
      ah, birdwind, puffs of ocean rinsing morning me
in silent flight eyewise cocked toward surf-face
      a string of seabirds streak the peeling line gawking
at sunbroken waves unhiding hundreds of fish in seaspill—
      watch: waves, fins, wings all silverbacked whitebellied
dive headfirst in rush thrush of splash, plumage, and gills
      quick keel and reappear as bobs in ocean yawn
surfing the moving moment of sea-spawn

I'm in the Ocean Spirit

in the dark storm the sea is seething
        churning up foam as white as spirit bear
                pelicans fight against nor'eastern wind
        but still they fly on the breaking waves—
I wouldn't be able to catch them
        too fast they rush and would crush anyone at Buxton
                trying to surf the crumblingPEAKS
        so I wade in the coldwinterwaters
and picture myself on calmer breaks—
        waves rolling in from a thousand miles away
                not these pushed by storm on shore—
        this is the thousandth morning I've come
to the beach to worship Spirit in motion

Cape Hatteras, Outer Banks, North Carolina

Whale Watching

for millions of years they roamed the oceans:
      behemoths braving waves, awesome leviathans,
seamonsters of the abyss who feared not even Yahweh
      in the primordial struggle for the control of earth's sea

a few northern hungry men hunted them in kayaks
      near the Arctic icebergs, harpooning their silvery backs
but when it was discovered they were rich in oil
      to light the lamps of Americans and Europeans
they were murdered to the brink of extinction

just now we see their miraculous resurrection—
      the sign of Jonah emerging from destruction—
they are filling the seas again and swimming free
      with spoutsOfJoy and flukesOf PelagicLiberty

to chase them around the Cape is so exciting
      in search of distant blowholes stoking—
"there she blows!" we all would yell in glee
      and then we'd see these massive monsters breeching
and gliding by our boat to look at us looking

they are now again masters of the sea—
the humpbacks, sperms, pilot, and greys!

Ocean Intruder

                    the ocean gray in the morning
usually catches some leftover light
from the moon
                    and there's always breaking
here and there some white churn which I slide down at eyes' height
                    beneath my feet
jacks dart blues dodge kings plunge
as I their surf intrude
                    paddling back I spot a mullet host
a gray ghost hovering on the green
popping jumping sliding whirling
the corralled won't leave their kind
fearing together is better
                    than escaping on their own.
slowly as the sun gallows in the hung mist
the commune is martyred
by invisible insidiousness—the jaws of ancient law
                    while I lay thin on my board
pretending to be invincible, watching the shade drift
now slimmer
than the horizon

Soaked

silversea turns mauve in greydawn
    flat as horizon flat as sky
        as I lay thin on my board and wait.
I cannot see but know the sun
    behind a veil of cloudsmear
        there is halfyellow in the air
        darkyellow in the waves
    as they curl peel drop disappear
    into ocean unscrolled across this stretch of earth
unsaying while waiting for some significance,
undisturbed except for plump pelicans diving thin
    and dolphins rocketing the surface
    exposed black to sun and rare to earth
        splashing flat and loud and down and gone
    into the deepgreen goinggray undertowed
as suddenthunderheads press the surface
    pushing a wilderness of waves my way
ghosting darkhooded bentover and brave
    through a million spears plunging individually
into water (more water than thirsty God)—
    all is wet all is water all is soaked
the sky the sea the air and me—
    then just as suddenly the skies depart
and I spot a wave swelling
    bluebodied bareheaded resurrected
from its grave of flattened gray
    I know that I must take it on
        or it will take me down

Climbing out of Water

the sea is roiledRollingCascading
        wave after wave rises and collapses
                (aquablue transforming into whitefoam)
        racing to their end with stallion speed—
manes flying in stiff offshore wind.
        the ocean is its own wild west
                with untamed creatures and unmanned features—
        she belongs to no one but wildGod
who roams this planet and millions more
        past suns and moons and seas and wind
                in a universe alive with frontier oceans
        pushing waves onto creaturelessCoasts
that will soon be captured by aquatics
        climbing out of water to crawl on land
                and one day evolve into a better kind of man

Caught in a Storm at Sea

strong seas, wind-whipped, swift spindrifts,
      colossalWavesmaverickWaveshumongousWaves
angry at everything, mad at nothing
      (God in the wild doesn't make sense)—
the fish beneath know nothing of the sea's face
      while the whales and dolphins have to surface
into an ocean rAging into rOilingRiOt
      having no mercy on any ship's pilot
trying to steer into the roller-coaster billows—
      the bow is pummeled, the deck is snowed
with crash after crash of breaking water—
      every wave rises on high like a tower
then crumbles into a h o l l o w e d-o u t trough—
      the spirit aches, the mind screams "enough!"
but the storm keeps pounding waves—
      there is no rescue, no one to save
I have to make it out alone

Ocracoke, Outer Banks, North Carolina

Riding Wavecrash

along the jagged horizon as in a Serengeti migration
the wind shoves a herd of waves hurrying ahead of storm

gusting a gaggle of waves, a swarm of surf in torrid downpour
deserting the sea to a watery wilderness pitching cresting falling

the only white in all this world is wavecrash foam and froth
the clouds, sea, sky, surf smear. mingle. mix in a world awash.

wind is rain and rain wind. no sun to tell the time. only the tide.
in all this drenched gray the only lumen is surfbreakingwhite

and flash of mackerel silver on the quick underside
chased by tigersharks dark with hunger, while I ride

the heave break snap curl of the hurling seabend
juiced with cloudbursts and surfers clinging on

to the pumped primed lunging sea flung and flattened
flung and flattened in seabend break and snap

wet with hunger wet with cold wet with wild waves
I don't surrender until much too much beach appears

Tasting Wind

fishless and thick with sea
    dark waves storm-wintered
stroke the shore with blackness
    and push every soul away
except a few blackgarbed surfers
    and one old man pushing a nor'easter

when the moon is long and sun thin
I forget the smell of sun and taste of wind

this flaw ends as suddenly as the seahawk snatch
    as quickly as the next catch of wave
glistening with glory in the curl and froth—
    these whiteheaded waves are the breaking of age
good for the young to ride and shout
    pleasant for the old to watch and contemplate

when the sun is long and moon thin
I remember the smell of darkness and taste of wind

Swanquarter

Traveling through Town

there is no clock
or town square
in Swanquarter
no church bells
ring the time
the same ol' cicadas hum
and bloodgorged mosquitoes bite—
the people who remain here
are replacements for the dead
with gravestones
already marked
on their foreheads
but they seem stayed with this
it's just the way it's always been
only the crabbers know
which pots among the hundred boxed stacks
browngreen with rotten seaweed
are good for catching and which are not

Croatan National Forest, North Carolina

I Toke Carolina Night

dripping through pipes immaculate
as Turkish opium thick and black
it falls as Carolina night and stains our air
with coats and coats of smokiness
settling late into the evening mind
suffusing, sedating, STRONGER than wine,
than sex, and l o n g e r t h a n f r i e n d s
conquering enemies and all that depends.
its sacredness I worship holy
and let it willfully take my body—
as it slurs my thoughts, steals what's tragic
I toke its thick MystiqueAndMagic.
it opiates anyone at any hour
king, culprit, crucified, or crucifier
it shouldn't be feared and can't be figured
it must revered as the sweet precursor.
Romans, robbed of it, died wide-eyed,
Americans, fighting it, exist deprived
no one can outlaw this soporific
it's drug divine, sanctioned paregoric

Discovering Spirit

I've found what I was not looking for
it was not the tall pine trees
reaching for the azure heavens
it was not the creeks running downhill
it was not the stones rounded by flow
transformed into variegated colors by the sun
it was not wildflowers visited by butterflies
who live only as long as summer
that saturates earth with blazing heat
it was not the moon that rules the waves—
it was the Spirit that permeates
all these livingthings and gives life
to trees, creeks, stones, sun, flowers, moon,
and it was in the butterflies that wave in wind

Hiding in These Woods

when they hunted you
        like dogs chasing rabbits
you hid in these woods
        alone with God and sun—
cloaked by tall pines
        you blanketed yourself with stars
ate wild roots and squirrels—
        deers became your brothers
as did wolverines and bears
        you avoided Wasuchis, your enemy
who believed in his manifest destiny
        but these trees were your sanctuary

Enjoying Precious Light

light is precious
a certain lean of light
soft, immaculate, unoppressive
making gentle fall
on the shadows of my eyes—
oh, what radiance in sight:
s l o w f o r e s t s u n s t r e a k s
spring leaves gleaming
after a storm has flattenedAndThinned—
isn't the light sweet and good
as good as God glowing
on flowerflocked meadows—
it's bright that almost blinds!
but then it bends and turns kindly
leading me to the path that ascends

Asheville, North Carolina

Finding Peace

deer bound softpawed through white aspen
       black bear claw rainbow trout from streams

all ears to the symphonic river
       that smooths rocks and signals sun
all eyes to the hungry hunted
       who escape the fleet, swoop, and tongue

an unburrowed groundhog spies enemies
       a magpie glides on upward draft

all ears to the snaredrum thunder
       that scares mares and spooks rain
all eyes to the hoarhead peaks
       that speak peace to those insane

With Us Still

not yet
no, not yet
still with us, thank God
you're with us still

while deers in the forest moan
deers driven to numb mountains
you are not ghost
still flesh and breath
yet with us, warm,
(bless Immanuel)

the wicked highway, bloodstained
curves around the groans

but angels silence us
angels moving quicker than deers
quieter than light
then disappearing into trees

while one body and only one
lies in the brown grass still

for John, after his car accident

Lookout Mountain, North Carolina

Enjoying A Sacred Moment

a sacred moment
just blew in with the western wind
the elm trees moved like water
the leaves sounded like river
as we ascended Lookout Mountain
into thinner air and thicker blue
we spoke of God breaking through the heavens
and speaking with us as with Abraham
but that was then, we concluded
as we moved around another bend
pausing now and again to enjoy the interplay
of shade and light on undulating glade

we climbed on, taking switchbacks here and there
unhurried we stopped to let some hikers pass—
you asked if the word was true
that all creation would be made new
to which I said, "the old will be removed
as far as the east is from the west"
then taking the lead again you swung around as aspen
and I, above the rush of clapping leaves,
barely heard you say "then we're new"

up we walked traversing rocks and fallen elms
circumventing a gnarly pine with exposed roots
to which I said "here's a tree that survived
and says to the world I'm here alive"
to which you replied "so am I"
as you took another step up

when we reached the height
we sought our own stone sanctuary
open only to the four winds and seven spirits
where under March sky and sun
God said something sweet and small
we laughed aloud and even howled
as we ran down that mountain trail!

for John

Black Mountain, North Carolina

Spring in Black Mountain

everylivingthing in the spring
runs
down
the mountain—
light tumbling
down rockface
snow melting
running streams
flocks of grass
herds of wildflowers
leaping rabbits
prancing deers
ranging wolves
and black bears
rolling out of caves
ambling around rocks
searching for anything
to bite and devour—
especially the she-bear
with twins
thinned by winter—
thinned by nursing
she rummages garbage
digs roots
raids anthills
licks sap
running
down
pines—
don't go up
against her
or her cubs—
she will
dismember
and you will
never ever
make it back up the mountain

Nantahala River, North Carolina

River Rafting

valleys hollowed between mountains
    scamper wet with wild rivers—
        and I get to paddle the one in this holler
    winding in white water cascading over rocks—
sun glistening on the overlooking cliffs
    river breeze fanning my face—
        if I kept stroking I'd flow into ocean
    mouth, swallower of all streams and rivers,
but for now I navigate the waves swelling,
    rising, chasing, propelling my raft
        down rapids strong as demons
    intent on turning, twisting, drowning anyone
crazy enough to surf a watery canyon

Pisgah National Forest, North Carolina

Viewing Valleys

verdant valleys running
   between plush mountains
stretching my imagination
   I am caught by your beauty
and want to write it in a book—
   as I scan from close to far
the mountains and valleys

they look like one scroll rolled tight
   then u n r o l l e d, followed by another
scroll rolled tight then u n r o l l e d
   and on and on, vellum after vellum
scripting an exquisite revelation
   of wave after wave—a perfect
inland ocean of hill and vale
   in rise and fall, in rise and fall—
mound, slope, trough, leveling off
   terrestrial peak after terrestrial peak
a sea of Carolinian majesty
   flowing on and on before my eyes
until I spot the glorious setting sun
   falling unfatal, unfinal, undone

Great Smoky Mountains, North Carolina

Climbing

steep steps up to ridge and crest
    around acacia sprouting from rock cliffs
        grabbing limbs to pull me upward
            loose shale crumbling under my feet
        I groan to ascend the heavingHeights—
    gasping, my breath fails me
like sun falling behind the mountain—
    climbing in opaqueness is dangerous.
        I pray to the moon for ascension
            and stars break and bloom open,
        bright lilies of the night sky—
    I keep climbing, head into heaven,
breathing heavier, believing my spirit can carry my body

Waiting the Parousia of Spring

night hangs a cold moon
and since the brown crusted leaves
have all fallen
the bare branched black elms
reaching to the cobalt blue heavens
feel the depths
of frozen roots
and iced veins
as dead
but since rooted
not moved—
brace against dark winds
and wait the parousia of spring
when the turned earth will flow again
and metamorphosis will come—
a brown chrysalis unfurling warm red wings

Linville Gorge, North Carolina

Awed by the Canyon

a stripe upon a canyon wall
      where rivers forced a sear
the tracing is not just and square
as limned by some carpenter
it dips
      jags
              disappears
merges with other lines
then reappears
        in different form
it bears no record of what has lived
only what has been

no one examining the wear
will note the stroke of being cut
      all groans are garbled in untold rush
downward to the sea, then hushed
        how
        mute
        were
        the
        deaths
        that
        forged
        these
        awful
        depths

Hammocks Beach State Park, North Carolina

Spotting Eagle and Solo Dolphin

usually out of sight, hiding in their own light—
      you have to be there, by luck, by God, at the right time—
right now one is camouflaged in the cypress branches
      it flashes into sight with bright white head
and elongated night-black wings flung into the air
      cruising on the updrafts sprung from the ocean
whirlingCirclingAscendingDescendingTiltingBending
      until it spots a whiting on the surface swimming—
it dives with wings tucked in and grabs it in its talons

nearby on the ocean side of this thin island
      I spot a solo dolphin as lonely as the moon
wishing it could join a constellation of its own kind
      gliding and sliding in and out of the deep ocean
in a pod that hunts schools of blues and plays in waves—
      I remember when several of them encircled me
as I lay on my surfboard a hundred yards out—
      they spokeGodintoMe and made me laugh
as I was calmed by their serene presence

Watching Dogs and Dolphins

butterflying so close to shore
I hear blowholes opening
into spontaneous revelation.
my golden retrievers hear them,
see them, want to join in play—
swimming with eyes open bright
into dawning sun that blinds
they chase a pod of dolphins
into the horizon where sea
and sky meet like two lips.

of all the creatures
only I have anxiety—
yet we are all animal:
the bald eagle
I eyed on the beach
clutching fresh flesh,
the sleek seagulls
cawing to God
winging the wind
above dogs and dolphins

for my two golden retrievers, Sunny and Myrtle

Enjoying Dolphin Soccer

Not much surf today, to speak of, rather slim—
       small knee-high waves pushed by southern winds.
I was about to paddle to shore when there appeared
       a pod of sleek dolphins, an epiphany of the sea
pushing out its best creatures like flowers into sun.
       I paddled out among them, an alien to eternal swimming,
drawn to these aqua angels who glideTheSeaLikeWind,
       who spirit the depths yet breathe, like me, oxygen.
As I lay on my board I pray they find me friend,
       not shark, not darkness, not shade, for I cannot tandem
with them. But there is a moment we share in our rare air
       before they slide back to sea and I stroke back to beach:
for a few moments we meet above the waters,
       even face to face—a sleek gray bottlenose with a grin
and I open-mouthed taking it all in, as he headed a jellyball
       flinging it, again, again ahead of him—sea soccer just for fun!

Fetching the Fetch

I see pearling waves come my way
I thrust my all to fetch the fetch
and catch the break furiously fast
to glide the ride at wave's pace
with all strength and touch of luck—
how awesome the sight (and light!)
when the wave opens before my eyes
into a wall of water before my board
which I race down, along open face—
this is the meaning of apocalypse:
the now of life better than then,
present presence, the flow of zen

nothing is fiercer sweet than presence
taking hold of spirit, aching, gripping,
an embrace, a kiss of the divine,
flowing, gushing a clean break,
flashing the mind, flushing the heart,
a find not asked for, parousia come,
the best of heaven on aqua earth.
like animal prance and bird climb,
the wave moves to its own rhyme—
a revelation of glorious face,
the grace of God for now and then,
no longer aching for Eden

Surf City, North Carolina

The Sun Breaches Ocean

on the horizon the sun breaches ocean
        emitting a whale of light—
light to swim in, light to breathe,
        light everywhere like life—
how precious to be among the living

but I wonder what would happen
        if the last dolphin swam greenSeas
the last macaw flew bright blueSkies
        what if the last tiger darkened the woods
the last ibex climbed craggy mountains?

what if the last field of grain waved
        the last tree plumped its sweet fruit?
what if only humans were left
        having murdered everything else?
what would it be to live in an unanimaled earth,
        a finless ocean under a flightless sky?

Breathing Spirit of the Ocean

       spirit of the ocean breathes
in rising and falling water
       making slim shallows
where godwits, oyster catchers,
       curlews, and turnstones wade
near seaside colonies of terns
       and rocky shores soaked in sunlight
beating down on seagulls and falcons.
       the coast is awash with thallasic sounds
of cawingSeabirds, breakingWaves,
       under the water are silent souls
scurrying on the ocean's bottom.
       from above the surf cormorants missile
into schools of mullets and blues,
       while deeper creatures cruise the depths—
lemon sharks, hammerheads, and squid.
       nothing is hidden from God's eyes
as he mingleswithSealife, flieswithSeabirds
       swims in benthic depths, watching bioluminessence

Hampstead, North Carolina

Surfing A Moment of Ocean

as clouds p a r t l i k e the Red Sea
and sunrise drops morning manna
        my blind eyes now see
it's like water changed to wine—
like leprosy falling off my skin
        as I dip in ocean
wild with heavy surf
warmed by southern winds

I swim until it's time to fly in my mind
skywide seafalcon into resurrection
and drink earth's glow sprung again

I breatheBreath of fresh Spirit
        s c a t t e r e d a l l a r o u n d
like sunlight on the beach
        I'm surfing on water—
                if even for a momentOfOcean

Witnessing an Epiphany of Sea

wild wind generated by rising sun
whips fierce waves into action
f e t c h i n g a c r o s s mighty o p e n ocean
they rise and fall, rise and fall
longer than any human dominion—
　　　in the end water conquers all

so brief is our earth existence—
macaws and eagles b r e a t h e l o n g e r
as do turtles swimming green seas
paddling past immortal jellyfish
floating aimlessly, mindless
of our nagging predicament:
　　　we believe we should not die

there is nothing more sacred
than waves rising in the sea
peeling and breaking down the line
　　　as they near Hampstead Beach

no grim eschaton is coming upon us
just more waves hallowing the coast—
　　　this is where people gather to watch God

Wrightsville, North Carolina

Being in This Moment

bluefish running fast
the gulls chasing minnows tell
fishermen fling their poles in hope of catch
while translucentCrosscurrentWavesCrash
in a wash of whiteAndCurl
        as for me this moment
I'd rather still and hear
the sound between waves
the sense between thoughts
the distance between lovers
as a sunny day turns suddenly gray

Imagining Myself As a Wave

as I scan the ocean this morning
        I imagine myself energy-born
                in a tropical storm
                        f e t c h i n g quite a d i s t a n c e—
                      strengthened by winds I RISE
              a rolling, roiling beast of power
        until all my force collideswithAsandbar,
is violently pushed upward,
        and into canyon-shape transforms.
              as I crest and barrel in roundness,
              as I featherPeelAndBreak,
        my colors run from rich lapis lazuli
to pale turquois, to frothy white and light!

Mystified by Majesty

like a shaman possessed
    by a holy spirit
the sea rises, dances, chants
    in whirlwind of water
towering higher and higher—
    like a forest of sequoias

I am overpowered by magic
    I am subdued by the invisible
forceful wind on sea—
    it is all greater than me,
        this MysteryofMajesty!

waves and waves never ceasing
    God's energy always e x p a n d i n g
the universe oceansforth
    never breaking on any shore
there are aeons of Ever more and more
    where waves rise but never fall
like light never caught by trees
    God speeds on for eternity

Enjoying Glorious Rides

the sun reveals super serene green surf
with glassy breaks p e e l i n g t o t h e r i g h t
      I paddle out on my board
and take some glorious rides
slidingdown head-high watery walls—
      peeling brightwhite behind me
like the insides of a melonrind revealed
when pared back—and I get the green fruit—
translucent green, sun-lit aquamarine waves!
      glorious waves! the best of God's creation—
t h e l o n g t h i n l i n e between turf and ocean

Viewing a Dance of Seabirds

the sun breaks the horizon
    and I see three flocks of seabirds
        weaving in and out of each other
            in rising and cascading waves—
            peeling and pearling, suddenly
      dropping as their wings stop flapping—
then rocketingUpward in one glorious burst
in one synchronized swoosh

in coordinated cadence they dance the sky
      to the musicOfTheSea percussing below
        doing what no humans could ever do
          as I stand on dry land wingless
          afraid of being buried in earth
        dreaming I could turn hands to pinions
      and quickly change direction
taking off into blueheaven

Getting a Message from Seagulls

the sky is bloodred, magenta over the ocean,
    drunk with the last outpouring of sun,
        the sea is also stained with blood
            as I watch a sandsharkchasemullets,
      circling, fins out, killing with each gulp
  whoever thought death could be so beautiful?
whoever imagined that death is life to others?

when I die I want God to eat me,
    or be swallowed in Jonah's whale,
        I hope he spits me out on some lonely island—
then I can watch the sea eternally

but for now I scan the graying horizon
    and spot seagull after seagull flying over me—
      they hover above for quite a while,
        swoopingGlidingFlappingCircling,
      flying in and out of each other as in a dance—
  they are messaging the divine to us,
telling us they are the higher species

Feeling Gusts

northeastGustsWhirl off the Outerbanks
pumping line-after-seismic-line of aqua waves
to our Carolina coast glistening
in the early risen sun
                                        winter is done—
spring has come: the sea smells so, the sky,
the magnolia blossoms breathing open,
the confederate jasmine climbing into my nose

God knows I've sprung alive into life
as I paddle out past the whiteBreakers
peeling from left to right, as I deep the sea
and see waves rising
                                        on the horizon—
duck diving, clinging to my wood, spitting sea water,
I'm thrilled to catch some superSlickrides
down some long lefts. I'm always amazed I ride a wave
and wonder if God gives fins for an old soul t o g l i d e

I wish I could do this a s l o n g a s thesunandsea
but I have only so many Springs to spring me,
more delicious as they pass, like drinking a cold
draught of apple juice
                                        after the grass is mown—
the quick coldness plummeting from tongue
to blood, liberating every thought for a moment,
so that for the time being it just feels so cool
to be a human being

I've been so thirsty for a drink of spring!

Carolina Beach, North Carolina

Studying Breaking Waves

clouds rise on the eastern horizon
like mountains hiding the ascending sun—
since their backside is bright
I believe in a God who hides
                but I wish he'd show his face
                                on the waves breaking my way

slowly the thin opening on the horizon
w i d e n s like an eye —and I feel watched

the eye is now wide open
beaming light on the ocean—
                its brilliant not to have any answers

sunlight cascades down the pillars
onto the sea like white waves
the color of ivory piano keys
                the sky is music

then just as quickly fog ghosts the coast
and I can't see anything but phantoms

Strolling under Ocean Sky

the sky explodes
with stars, endless stars
some of these will die
and become supernovae—
from these we're born nouveau
        we're made of stars' stuff—
                we are the universe
                        and the universe is us!

this is our significance—
small as we are
we are large with cosmic life
that was released
by a wild Spirit God
        billions of years ago
                in a swirl of mystery
                in a flash of majesty
that keeps breathing
        pneumaZoePsuche
                into all the zoa
                in millions of earths
                        brimming with oceans
                                pumping green waves

Carolina Beach State Park, North Carolina

You Were Ready

as I stroll the beach and gaze at the sky
I remember how we wanted you to stay
so you struggled on and on
to please your wife and sons
but in your heart of hearts
in your deepest spirit
you knew it was time to depart—
you were like a chrysalis stirring
just waiting for the cocoon to split apart
so you could fly to God like a monarch
in the ocean winds of eternity
forever free of pain and mortality

in remembrance of my father—a poem I read at his funeral

Making Ocean Incantation

the ocean's incantation is tantric to my ear
magicMantraMotion turns the wheel of prayer

the sea is breathing deeply and I'm inspiring
the celeritous cycle cleansing all desiring

as the body of the sea releases its living chi—
eternal energy flows kundalinic in me

ubiquitous voice echoing from shore to shore
there is more to hearing God than mystic lore

today I feel like I'm one with Buddhist prayer
desiring nothing more than to be here

Rising Resurgent

the sea rises tide after tide
in refluent resurgence:
in sempiternal seriation
     wave after sinuous wave
         strikes/staccato/on/the/shore—

there is more resurrection
in this ocean than I can imagine

its fullness breathes and overruns
as its vast body rises
diurnal from its depths
     I feel the eternal recrudesce
         and fill my lungs with breeze and song—
there is more transformation
from this ocean than I can imagine

Bald Head Island, North Carolina

Walking in Soft Sea Fog

I watch the soft sea fog blur the sea rocks' contours
        as the skyAndSea's grayMistMingle offshore,
and I hear the sea's voice in the surge of rising tide
        creating a tumult of watersounds, swashings, swirlings—
a perpetual slapping against the rocky rim of land
        with undertones of murmurings and whisperings,
suddenly obliterated by the water's torrential inpouring—
        all because the bloated moon is aligned with the sun.
the springtide (*sprungen*) has impregnated the ocean
        to brimmingFullness with stronglong movement
of surges leapingAndDancing over jutting rocks
        in long cascades of foam spilling on the edges

in the recurrent rhythms of tides and surf,
        the long rhythms of planet sea on planet earth,
the marl has been sculptured in bays and cays
        by sea forces pressing forwardRecedingReturning—
the sea's edge perpetually reclaimed by the rising tide
        bringing food for flamingos, sanderlings, and gulls—
the ebb exposing the long prop roots of mangroves.
        as landAndSea interchange their lives, the coast
is constantly transformed from face to face—
        and I imagine it once a lovely unpeopled place
where darknessRuledNight, moon was the only light,
        and days were a s l o n g a s l o n e l y b e a c h e s

Moved by Wind Spirit

wind spirit, you move sea.
walk waves. plunge hurlers into flesh,
flashPeelCrushCrash.
      they spirit away
like so many other holy ghosts I've rode.

you phantom water, incarnate curls and bends.

      you open sun and close like purple rose at dark.
you lift stars. you drift, shape-shifter,
      sea-lifter. you drip, drenched. cool.

I've caught your face.
unveiled. lifted. smooth. serene,
when and only when you show yourself
      then speed away. still,
wind spirit, you return unpredicted.
unwritten. apocalyptic.
      seizing the skies, you make earthrise.
sunbend. cloudfall.
waterless hands await you. cupped.
      dry mouths open. unearthed
           mourners looking for souls.

you come to drums. by dances.
through flutes. in songs.
      you are muse and music. blend
           poet and oracle. shape and shifter.
shade and light, wavetop bender.
      the slender inbetween. take flight,
           sender of dreams, make light monarchs' wings

and go, going away. good God,
wind spirit, what have you brought?
      long memories of oceans.
           of sailors. of lovers lost.
               the deep couldn't hold you back?

moans must you carry? cross?
seized moments. the last drops.

I've lost your voice, wind spirit,
      in louder pains of flesh. attack.
            pierce. I'm hollow. your lute. sing.
the prophet bends. send word.
gust. make me spirit too.
      make me flesh of you. open. crack

the dawn. pump everliving breath.
      breathe in me and I am soul.
let go and I am sand.
dust. earth. dry. dead. forsaken. limp.
      a lump. O, fuse. force. be fierce.
         my firmament fill. flash. flood.

wind spirit, I am gashed. poured.
      watered. wet. winded. liquid.
melted. you undress me.
      make me holy. ghost ungone.
         I am spirit. unborn. undead.
            flow. muse and music. beyond

and in. over and through.
there is not end. beginning. just you,
wind spirit, lifebreath, quickening verve,
      sustaining wings, limbs, and lips. guts and gall.
         voice, call, coo, and crow. carrion
            is not you. nor anylivingthing.
               light of eyes. sap of flower. sing

and song. move and movement.
wind spirit, I am longing to be
      rent and sent. given and gone.
         coming and going. flung and fling.
slimmer. quicker than God gone to ghost

and wind gone to wave

wind spirit, you slip between the earth
      and silence. over barriers of sound.
            you are round. always round.
               never gone, good giver.

Emerald Isle, North Carolina

Catching Ghosts of Water

I caught the earthrise sun this morning
    in a slit between two sheaths of clouds
one hanging on the water like a lover
    the other hanging from the sky like a thief.
as the sun passed through these, it lingered
    just long enough in between to mean something.
I snatched this sign and ran it to the sea
    where I surfed the day bywavesbystorm,
as ghosts of water fell on breaks and peaks
    turning them velvet, soft, supple, sheen.

the green sea breaks constantly
into white waves looking like the clouds
    ambling down the shoreline
both are moving—the celestine and marine
mirroring and coloring each other,
waves and clouds, water and water,
    the stuff of life, the stuff that matters

none of it is solid, like my spirit, my ghost, my angel

I can't soar where they fly just yet
but one day I will unbody, I will exit
    and traverse the great mysteries—
the bottom of the abysmal sea
    the heights of our swirling galaxy
I want to fly like a sea falcon
dive in free fall and clutch in my talons
    the meaning of the dark wriggling ocean

North Myrtle Beach, South Carolina

Dreaming of Waves

I see the waves are good for surfing
      which I enjoy for an hour or two
but I trudge out of the sea thinking I had just surfed waves
      I had dreamed and not the waves that just had been.
I can tell you about them—they were headhigh, gnarly,
      driven by straight eastern wind as before a hurricane
but when I came out of the water after the last wave
      I didn't know if I had stepped out of water or dream—
one of those from my menagerie of weird waves
      I've ridden in backyards, highways, viaducts, tunnels,
creeks, inland and out, in winter and in heat

perhaps I'm just as much dream as the reality
      of what I've done and am—two beings both each other,
the seen and the seer, facing each other strangely familiar

Having a Beach Dream

I fall asleep on the beach and dream a vision
    where I am floating or flying—
it feels like I have no body
    yet I must have feet, hands, and eyes
because I am walking in paradise
    and see the God I always wanted to see—
he is life whoLivesIntheLiving,
    who breathesMovesIsAlwaysIs,
is always beginning, never ending.
    his home is not in heaven only
but everywhere, so much like earth,
    an abode of the living zoa—
lions, eagles, oxen, men,
    spirits, angels, and cherubim
full of eyes and sprouting wings;
    an ocean churns at his feet,
a river flows from his throne
    on whose banks grow fruit trees.

    I listen to the waves breaking –
a sound like harpists strumming.
    I hear rivers tumbling over rocks,
and he himself looks like jasper
    encircled by an emerald rainbow.
where he is there is brilliant light
    and flowing water—everywhere is God,
is life; his light colors everything
    from heavens to new earths in the universe.
oh yes, now I see the Creator,
    the maker of new heavens and earths.
and I realize he still creates
    breath, life, spirit, bones,
waves, trees, flesh, stones,
    grass that grows, flowers that bloom,
eyeballs, fishtails, talons, wings,
    and forests creeping with creatures.
all is moving in this universe

like the waves of the seas,
stars are exploding, galaxies swirling—
spirit flows from his mouth, breath
that quickens, color that thickens,
as he paints sunrises and sunsets,
marshes, swamps, jungles, and woods.
all is alive with the ichor of God.
his life is pulsating through the veins
of animals, insects, birds, and men,
lions, bears, cheetas, zebras;
nothing can MoveOrBreathe without him.
even death is his, the grave undertaker,
for GodIsSpirit that can't be killed—
all goes on living in another world.

Wacammaw Indian Reserve, South Carolina

Attending a Pauwau

the drummers beat the drum in unison
with the life-beat of the heart of earth
and offer GrandfatherGod festive songs
whose living Spirit saturates the dancers
ringing the sacred circle around the sacred fire—
their bright colors swirl, their feathers fly
in the wind flowing through their bonnets
as they celebrate their ancient tradition
OfBeingOneWithAllThingsBreathing
who constitute a wonderful circle of life
infused by God, good giver of mana—
the smiles of the women tell beautiful stories
the faces of the children shine like sun
there's nothing on earth like this celebration!

Myrtle Beach State Park, South Carolina

Watching Surfers

the sea is glass, a pond to skate on
a mirror for the sky's changing faces.
young tanned men come and go to shore
with waxed boards and fluid memories
but tideAfterWatchedTide drops their mood
like the half-lit moon in the west
but so does the pressure
              the ground s l o w l y swells beneath the sea
bumping up substantial successive ridges
a southwestern holds them firm and strong
as they move along, rising higher and thicker
until they peak and trim a h u n d r e d y a r d s l o n g
each wave peelingDroppingPearling
as if some invisible finger slid down an ivory keyboard
              but the sound is not piano—it's percussion
tight snare roll, zildjian crash, morocco sizzle
as the surf breaks and stallions toward shore
past darting mullet and scampering sandpipers
to the ankles of these bronzed islanders
bound to the sea and the board that takes them
beyond the chop, breakers, and roll
              where they watch the culmination
of arduous African migration
storm-swelled o v e r f a r f e t c h e s
wallAfterLiquidWall moves toward shore
as the surfers take off in fierce anticipation
of the thrill of standing under that curl
that can thrust or crush the interloper
who dares to call himself surfer

Garden City Beach, South Carolina

Having an Epiphany

as I am paddling out to catch a wave
    in bright sunlight thrown about by southern winds
        I have an epiphany

it is but a breath
    slim as shadows that flatten as I near
        thin betweenHereandThere as a spider's web
        as ink upon papyrus sheets
    that flecks off with slightest touch—
yet it reads so significantly

it has no form but I have seen it
    no weight but I have held it
        like sky stretching out the day
            it is a thin whisper of sound
            the monarch's antenna tuned
        to the sun escaping clouds
    it is the breathing spirit of nature
where breathing o u t is breathingIn

I slide into this quiet presence
    of crystalline light cradled between waves
        an ocean o p e n i n g like butterfly w i n g s
    I ascend a shaft of sunlight
to surf the break until it ghosts a w a y

Huntington Beach National Park, South Carolina

Looking at a Sea Acacia

there were times of singing but it has been way too long
   since then, way too deep hide the vowels of joy
for me to well them up again. they were there once
   I remember, I recall singing, I remember joy and the taste
but my tongue is soaked with saltwater, my heart soused with wine
   my bones are shaking, my fingers tremble on broken rhyme
my pen moans like a broken vessel warped by slanted seawind

in the ancient waters I see long spirits rising and dying
   invisible horses churning the waves, angels treading water
onto the broken shore where a sea acacia with sea limbs
   crooked by gnarly winds holds terra firma only as long as . . . . .
you've outsung me, old man, but not the sea of winds.
   the ocean always wins; it won't paean you or me
as we seagreen and our roots topple upsidedown

Litchfield Beach, South Carolina

Sensing the Soft

the sea is soft in an offshore wind
    the sun is soft partly veiled by clouds
        the sand is soft as it squishes beneath my toes
    the sky is soft filled with a thousand seagulls
weaving in and out of each other in flight
    quicklyRisingDivingShifting to the right
        and left as they enjoy their wings in wind.
    their areal dance clouds the horizon,
synchronizing their black-tipped wings
    they swiftly riseTurnTwistDrop
        as if they were one creature of God—
    how incredible their unified motion!
how wonderful their symbiotic union!

North Pawleys Island, South Carolina

Watching a Rescue

the sun pulled the windy sky into a dive
        of maroon splattering the horizon
the full moon followed like a victor's horse
        dragging a host of vanquished stars
towing a swollen sea into the northern inlet
        dumping whitecapped billows
into a turgid creek ripping round our island

as the tide surged and undertow sucked
        where ocean and inlet mingle
the water jumped turned twisted and growled
        old leviathan resuscitated

there we stood next to this awesome denizen
        a few feet from certain drowning
while sirens wailed LouderThanTheRoar
        fingers started pointing and eyes strained
a crowd began to gather muttering ultimate questions
        no one could hear above the booming surf
as rescuers strapped in orange life-vests
        sped into the inlet one craft after another
looking deep for the boy who tried to cross

Pummeled by Long Strong Sea

I woke and wanted to surf
     but the ocean is so long strong
with waves more powerful than my bones
     I battle wind, I fight peaks
but the force is mightier than me
     I am pummeled and swallow sea
I am tumbled and fall to my knees
     I ride a wave on my belly into shore
furiousFroth churning behind me
     dejected that I was beat by the ocean—
she is the ultimate conqueror on earth—
     when she is moved by potent winds

Surfing a Riot of Waves

I have surfed with them after squalled suncast,
      in a flush of torrentTreading the beach
bending palms, winging from the northeast,
      where wetness completely wraps the earth—
yes, we have surfed a riot of waves

I have surfed with them when the sky is peace
      and the sun is brisk until it slowly crawls to dusk,
when the waves are cleanAndBreakingOpen
      like cotton scattered in the wind chasing us
down the face of bliss and laughter

I have surfed with them the tonic sea in tall winds,
      slidingdown glacis, glidingSmoothAndSerene.
I never want it to stop, and they don't tire of being with dad
      as my shouts mingle with the air: "Nice ride!" "Cool turn!"
and we paddle back out for more

For my sons, Peter and John

Paddling out with Friends

Though it used to be, I'm told, one of the few
       East Coast competition spots, Pawleys Island
isn't world-class surf. But some days it's epic.
       And many days good enough for we locals
who know what to look for and when—
       by tide, pier, groin, by wind, storm, moon.
We'll get pounding nor'easters WinterIntoSpring,
       and we'll have them all glorious to ourselves
till summer surf comes with inland vacationers
       and lots of new faces taking occasional breaks
pumped by thunderstorms and southwest winds.
       All of them exodus before autumn springs for us
anew with tropicalSwells and hurricaneSurges—
       the swollen ocean all pregnant with waves!

It's festal to paddle out in May with friends,
       some to the north and some to the south of the pier:
the goofy-footers taking peeling lefts, the longboarders
       waiting outside to catch stretched-out lines,
the shortboarders rippingCuttingSpinningSpraying—
       while I prefer to s l i d e r i d e g l i d e.
No matter. All of us glow and brim with the hollering sea
       and wear ourselves out like flattened beach.
That night when I close my eyes for sleep, I see swell after swell
       rise, form, peel, churn, surge, crash, mush, foam.
And I catch faces of waves and friends in the surging sea—
       epiphanies of Creator Spirit flowing fresh and free.

Touching a Beached Whale

the sea was swelling and rolling oh so gently
    until the late afternoon when it whipped up strongly
        and pushed to shore a creature from the depths—
            a sperm whale nearly twenty feet in length

we kept wondering when it would return to sea
    but it kept heading toward Pawley's shore
        and then beached itself in the shallow surf
            wavesCascadingandCrashing on its dark body

none of us, with all our combined strength,
    could coax her back to the waters of life
        I patted her gray skin and looked into her eyes
            I could tell—we all could—she'd come here to die

it broke my heart to watch her gasp and fade
    when she had once been mistress of the ocean—
        no human could save her from destruction
            just as no one can ever change the tide's direction

Afraid of a Gator in the Ocean

in all the years I've surfed Pawleys Island
      this is a first: an alligator swimming in the ocean
next to schools of mullets flipping in the air
      chased by my retrievers until they spot the gator
and swim after him, jaws open wide—
      on the outside past the breakers of the ocean
another school of mullets are being corralled
      by a pod of streamlined bottle-nosed dolphins
who porpoise up and down and circle round
      taking turns to gorge themselves on their prey
and then the seabirds make their parousia known—
      seagulls, pelicans, sea falcons cry to the wind
and divebomb into the green pelagic main
      filling their slender gullets with squirming mullets

the gator disappears beyond the breaking whites
      and is lost to sight as he swims to the deeper side
my swimming retrievers can't site him yet
      even though they keep straining their necks—
he's swimming dark waters in long mystery
      when leviathans once ruled the roiling sea

later I return to the ocean
      and there is absolutely nothing
but a creatureless mass of water moving
      no gator, no mullets, no seabirds, no dolphins
not even any sun, as gray masters the day
      and I am alone

South Pawleys Island, South Carolina

Remembering Her

I remember all the mornings on the south island
when you swam the channel to the other side
your nostrils flared, your four feet kicking
Sunny was always just behind you swimming—
he returned soon, you lingered and hunted
looking for anything moving and alive
when you swam back you dug for ghost crabs
clawing a hole deeperAndDeeperAndDeeper
Sunny barking until you grabbed your prize
then the two of you would runAndRunAndRun
into the sun, into the shallows, into tide pools
two golden retrievers alive as in elysian fields

so to see you laying there fully paralyzed
unable to move any of your precious legs—
having been slammed and run over by a truck
was the worst luck, a tragic sudden death
a pain I can never erase from my mind.
I pray for the day, Myrtle, we will run again
down the sun-sprayed beaches of paradise—
never again—no, never again—to face the end

in memory of my last golden retriever, Myrtle

Hunting the Elusive Fugitive

primed waves pitch, plunge, drop, roll
    past my retrievers chasing slippery pelicans
winging into the dark dusked sun
    I'd hurl evanescence's preciousness
if I could immutable hold—
    or do I yearn for everlasting transience
the elusive fugitive, God?
    nonlinear, unchronicled, the push to places
of the mind, the near fulfillment of dreams
    grasped, lapsed, words come true, not truer
all language explored, exhausted, spirit

creamwhite magnolia blossoms crushed in the palm
    the fragantFlash. sweet. gone.
dreams gripped in dark slipping through the crackofDawn
    suns you swear you saw
oceans I slid into and out dripping with God.
    there is sadness in the taking,
a lack of movement to the celestial wheels
    rotating, girating. the goggling
of seven eyes of seven spirits watching the wicked
    wear this world. (enough.)
I'm tired of running for rest. There must, there has
    to be a page after the book
a sound after cymbal's crash, another explanation

that there's nothing
    mindful after us. Yes, I've heard owlhoot, frogcroak,
dogbark, dovesong
    say nothing significant and say it all—it doesn't end
with bang or whimper.
    it just doesn't end. never mind the long explanations.
I'm gonna live forever because I think
    in the long swoop of God
and arch of angels there's a hallowed peace of earth
    primed for children
laughing innocent and pure, seeing him invisible
    visage of us all. And then

Thirsting

the sun throats in its burning
in a billion years it will gulp desert-earth

thirst is a strange creature
it is the wanting to be living

I thirst
sometimes I don't know what for—
to swallow new earth, drink a planet
pure as liquid God

then thirst is good
it is the wanting to be living

the moon moans in its mooring
soon it will be unanchored and freed
to float wherever

there goes our sea swallowing earth
but never can it swallow thirst

I will not compare you to sun
I will not say you're moon
or imagine you're ocean

stronger than ocean
longer than sun
fuller than moon

life is the mightiest thirst

Scanning Seawaves and Seabirds

I see a wave quickly lift off the horizon on the sea
   like a thick flock of seabirds rocketing into flight suddenly—
    flappingandTrimming off to the right of the beach
    (close enough to wonder, but just beyond my reach)
   swoopingandSallying then swiftlyDropping
cascadingFrothingandLanding back into the flat ocean

on the beach I watch a swarm of seagulls rise
   looking like a humongous wave touching the sky
     coloring the horizon with gray and white wings of wind.
     and then the flock descends like a cascadingWaveofOcean
   back to flat stillness—a pond of seabirds resting,
waiting for the next flash of fish chased by dolphins

and seabirds make my world mystical—
   always moving, rising, cascading, thin then full.
    flocks of waves, waves of flocks, shape-shifting
     from bodies to spirits, not earth-bound, but lifting—
   they ascendTranscendTransport and free my soul
from the defeat of my feet, from the weariness of being old

Reveling in the Loggerhead Mystery

after years of swimming the Sargasso seas
      they head out into the dark green deep
migrating toward the island where they were born
      directed by Spirit through pelagic calm and storm
they wait until the beach is vacated of souls—
      deep into the black night they paddle ashore
and lumber up the sand to the sea knolls
      where they dig with their flippers very deep holes
and deposit hundreds of white slippery ovum
      then shuffle their way back to black ocean—
all summer long the eggs lay hidden
      slowly maturing under the yellow sun.
I have walked right by them on the beach
      unaware of what treasures were under my feet
under moonlight in cool late September.
      the neophytes hatch and dig into night air
and scamper like crazy toward the rushing surf—
      like every turtle has done since their birth.
hungry seagulls and falcons pick off many—
      then they have to hide from other enemies.
if they can make swim to the Sargasso waters
      they can live long—almost a hundred years.

the mysteries that move the creatures of the sea
      pass my understanding—are way beyond me

Making the Beach His

the beach is his. he makes it. the darting minnows
   in surge, suck, sally. the sandpipers scurrying
   between swooshes. the dallies with clawing crabs.
the pelicans bobbing on the sea like sun.
the swim, the search in crushed waves for the stick I pitched.
the fetch, prance, strut—like a majorette, he waves the stick
   as high in the air as he can get it.
             he is good so good. it is his universe.
those who stroll by sense, catch, smile, and share the glow
   as we kick our way through the shallows
northwardheaded—I with board in hand and he with stick in jaw—
   and slosh our way to the northern spit
where I begin to surf nor'eastern shifts and slide winddown
   southbound breaking lefts, all the while trailed
by my companion who watches my catches and follows my drift—
excited by every ride, he runs along, my terrestrial shadow.
and even if I mingle with a swarm of other blackgarbed surfers
   he stays fixed on me until I ride the last wave to shore
where I am met in the shallows by the sweetest soul
   with dance, swagger, primal joy, contagious happiness
he wants more. so much more. never to leave the surging sea—
   to chase dogs, rays, and falcons, to fetch, catch anything called life
   but I exhausted soaked and spent, coax him toward the exit,
where we pass many a local who don't known my name
nor I theirs, but they call out anyway: "Hey, Charlie! how's the surf?"

for my golden retriever, Charlie

Surfing with Surfdog

the sun breaks the horizon
      and glows with God's glory
about to make the day's story.
      the two of us paddle out—
I on my long surfboard
      and Charlie right next to me

when we finally get out
      to where the waves bump up
he puts his paws on my board—
      I get off and help him up
there we wait for a good break
      watching seabirds take off,
land, and bob on the ocean
      listening to breaking waves
percussing on the shore

then all of a sudden
      I see a good one coming
I push him into the wave—
      he rides it, sitting sphinx-like,
in all his canine glory
      gliding all the way to shore
where several beachgoers cheer.
      and then we go out for more

for my golden retriever, Charlie

Beautiful Ride

A beauty is coming. I hesitate for a second,
thinking the other surfer down the line will get it,
but I realize he's letting it pass for me.
I paddle hard, looking over my left shoulder
at the wave forming gorgeously. I take it
at its peak and make the drop by leaning back
on my board and then immediately forward
as I'm launched across the face of a gracious wave
that stays held up by the offshore zephyr
for longer than any I remember—
as I glide along eyeing this headhigh hyaline
I realize I'm face to face with miracle in motion,
as close to the quick of creation as I may ever be;
my heart is beating out my mouth
my mind is screaming, "this is my longest ride ever!"—
this wave that is long and sleek, strong and steady,
a beauty of a beast that moves me all the way to shore,
where I dismount my board and sit in awe,
trying to recapture as quick as I could
the sweetest, longest wave I've ever surfed.

Experiencing Twin Hurricanes

wild daughter of Neptune,
Marie, the hurricane,
spins ferociously fast
off the south California coast
pumping gorgeous sets
twenty-five feet tall
cascading into humongous falls
that watermen can't recall
happening for dozens of years—
body surfers, boogie boarders
and long board surfers
take off at the wave's brim,
fall airborne and skim
across the speeding face
at "ball's out" pace—
only to crash in the break
that crushes those who mistake
the ocean for a friend—
some those days met their end

another crazed daughter of Poisedon,
Cristobal, the hurricane,
started in the Caribbeans
spinning along the Atlantic coast
pumping nor'easter sets
from Florida to Maine
in counter-clockwise motion—
four days in a row
I went to the beach and saw
raging nor'easter monsters
that I wouldn't dare encounter
but on the fifth morning
waves were gloriously forming
way out on a sandy reef
so I paddled out to the break
and waited anxiously for a set
to rise and roll my way—
I got in a good place and got lucky
to catch and ride a gorgeous beauty!

Hurricanes Marie (west coast USA) and Cristobal (east coast USA)
August, 2014

Pawleys Island Creek and Marsh, South Carolina

Admiring Angels of the Marsh

angels of the marsh soar
    on cherubic wings and float
        as if heaven were their boat
    (such a large wing span
for such a thin light frame).
        as they flap they sing guitar—
            a guttural bass deep in the throat
        uttering clear distinct notes—
I wish I could translate their tongue
        but maybe it's better I am dumb
            so they can have their world to themselves
        as do the angels, the zoa, and everything else
that inhabits heaven's glorious realm—
        since we are intruders in their world
let us paddle gently and not say a word

dozens of them perch on a Carolina oak
        overlooking the marsh in tide waters soaked.
            dozens more tiptoe in the shallows
        hunting quietly for blues and minnows—
their bright golden eyes look left and right
        searching for the fish they will strike
            they silently stalk what moves in the creek
        nabbing the fish in their orange beaks—
and then they begin another long wait
        whether in wind, in sunshine, in wet.
            they are masters of meditation
        who can outlast any Zen
Buddhist in his protected pagoda—
        the snowy egrets know God and zoa
            and the spirit creatures of heaven,
        for they are the most like them—
even moreso than the sons of men.

Kayaking the Sea Creek

Mirroring mackerel skies, flocculate clouds, sun so bright
it shouts, a cirrus seacreek annulates Pawleys Island,
    a corolla round a cay that's been hurricaned
to death and resurrects. Each sunrise is breath.
The oscillating tide pushes the creek high, pulls it low
    in pulmonary flow, sucking sea air into its throat,
    exhaling a scent so pungent it's poignant.
I sit creekside hearing breaking waves off to my east,
waves that have beached spermwhales, buried billions
    of unsouled shells, broken bodies into sand,
and hurled at man more mysteries than explanations.
    On a sunworn dock reaching into this savannah,
I admire a swallowtail hanging summersun on amaranth
its wings shutting, papyrus pressed, and flinging open
an aperture into ever slowness. A bullfrog not about
to move the day bellows in sawgrass not hurrying sun
or shade, as yonder I eye a gator gliding as quiet as time,
his stare never aging, his eyes not fearing that I am.
    I spot a goldeyed snowy egret ghosting forward
with slow step in silent shallows bending its sigmoid neck
in half a circle; the other penciled by imagination.
It's all a slow circle drawn diurnal,
a continual annulating in euphotic waters where
acropetal circles appear everywhere from nowhere.
I didn't throw a stone or cast a line or dip my toe.
And there were no raindrops I could feel.
My thoughts drift into shades of brown smeared across
the marsh lit by summersun burning out the cusp of day.
    Does anything here imagine anything else?
I wish I had no other mind as I sit here watching
lightfall spring native night, moonshadows crawl around,
and stars birthed in some novae billion lightyears past
just now being grasped.

Ocean Highway 17, South Carolina

Roadkill Requeim

for the flattened fox
whose tail still wags in the highway wind
for the smeared skunk gut-spilled
the squashed cat and splattered squirrel
    say something for them in solemn tones
for the gushed crow-pecked groundhog
the mangled rabbit in dried blood
the decapitated snake and wasted wren
    the unconvicted must pray something anguished
for the eviscerated deer with stunned eyes
the stiff-legged dog and dumb opossum
    say something for the unburied unburrowed masses
who've died while making natural crosses
on roads that are death rows for the innocent
(and we are not at all penitent)
    but let's pray Ezekiel to slip from the dead
and breathe into their gaping jaws
that they may earth our forests again
    O God!

Ode to the Vulture

you are majestic in flight
    kettling high in upward drafts
        winding in circles searching for death
    the native Americans venerated you
the Zoroastrians worshipped you
    because you picked clean the flesh
        of their mortal relatives
    laid out for sky burial on trees and roofs
you eat what no one craves
    feasting on rotten meat and marrow
        like Shiva, you take death away from earth—
    for this you should be honored
not hated, despised, and abhorred—
    one day you will tear apart my tendons
        and separate my flesh from my thighs
    liberating me to wing with your kin on high
releasing spirit that never dies

Wacammaw River, South Carolina

Sensing a Certain Presence

every living river exudes a certain presence:
    in the infinitude of the moment
liquid quiddity passes into consciousness,
    aquatic apotheosis oozes, an aura glows,
and its quintessence flows unutterably real,
    quiet as sunrise, and quick (it can't be caught)
nor can it be lost on those who know
    and touch the revelation in person—
it's like feeling water pass through to the next
    moment of now; it's animal, primal, unfinal,
palpable for an instant until another present is

River Dolphins and Eagle

wet fog suffuses the island
 all is ensconced in spirit mist—
  the sea, the sky, the beach, and us
   we await sunlight to be our savior
  but then we see seagulls appearing
 out of nowhere, winging southwest,
we follow them to the Wacammaw River
 where, to our surprise, we spot dolphins
  porpoising in the water and spouting air—
   then—o spirit—an eagle soars overhead
  making us shout with delight, grin,
 and thank Almighty Spirit for this sign

for my grandson, Reid

Listening to Watersound

too much is made of meaning, too little is wrung from sound
rhyme is defunct, uncool, rhythm untapped and snared
moderns can't hear rivers carving canyons
seas sanding shores
continents shifting in water
glaciers moving poles
(their sound signifies nothing)
but it is not noise—no—when spheres sing to spheres
and deep calls to deep in language we can't fathom
the motion is music
the music is word
the word is spoken
when the speaker can be heard
it slithers Wacammaw and Catawba curves
it creeps savannah slowly under the utter sun
as rivers become oceans and seas become poems

Standoff between Golden Retrievers and Brown Cottonmouth

wouldn't say it was a war
between good and evil
but it sure looked like it—
my two golden retrievers
barking into the heavens
surrounding a cottonmouth
who had found his way
into the dunes next to the river.
And I wouldn't say I was God
but I thought I had the power
to determine the outcome
of the war between these creatures
who instantly became enemies—
mind you, there wasn't any hatred
in battle over land or religion,
just primordial struggle for survival.

None of them was about to back down—
the dogs kept barking and circling,
the snake kept turning and lurching.
I kept waiting for them to go in for the kill.
Surely their jaws were stronger, I reckoned,
there was two of them to one;
they had killed ghost crabs, sting rays,
possums, squirrels, black snakes, rabbits;
yet this cottonmouth was something else,
somehow they sensed she had poison—
now where had that come from?
from the same God who made good and evil?
No wonder Zarathustra created Ahura Mazda,
but Nietzsche was wrong to have the prophet
proclaim "God is dead"—my dogs knew better
as did the cottonmouth who quickly wriggled off.

for my two golden retrievers, Sunny and Myrtle

Debordieu Beach, South Carolina

Grieving the Day My Son Moved

the ocean is salty this morning

    so are my tears

mercurial, silvergray, expensive ink
spills across a parchment page
before the damp sun broke

    so does my heart

Africanoarange and Africanwinds shimmer the sea

    we shared exotic dreams

the waves peel down the line
pumped by a distant hurricane

    your leaving rips me

I paddle out and take another peeling right
and then another, and still another
until my shoulders ache, legs cramp

    and I am crushed

again I paddle out
and wait with others for another set
driven by Caribbean wind

    not knowing what I'm thinking

as we watch half a rainbow arch
climb to heaven but not bend down

    half our hopes are broken

as the sea begins to calm
and turns inkblue, running
soft across the parchment page

primed and presaged

for Jeremy

Hagley Estates, South Carolina (my home)

Staring at a Gator in My Backyard

an alligator is staring at me with eyes
as old as Moses, as Arabian deserts,
as spirosaurus swimming ancient rivers—
he is staring with eyes as greenAsSea,
as newborn turtles, as grass never mowed,
with eyes as still as a sphinx, as a tiger
crouching before a kill, as a spaniel pointing,
as slaves being photographed near the shed,
as dead Confederate soldiers wide-eyed at Antietam,
as a judge pronouncing a sentence of death—
I am forced to look away in denial
that I have just seen the leviathan Job saw
who was God's answer to why there's pain

Saving Drowning Insects

I have a ritual summer mornings:
I try to save drowning insects.

I scoop out bloated cockroaches,
        mosquitoes thin as nothing, dreaded horseflies,
        scads of no-see-ums, southerners' perennial enemies,
        now defanged, undangerous, limp as wet tissue.
                I ponder the paradox of intelligent design
                (why are those intricately made so irritating?)
as I palm brown moths and toss them over the side,
        I wonder why I've never seen a butterfly drown.
They're angels of the insect world I conclude,
as I continue to be more funerary than salvatory.

I accumulate a cadre of corpses:
dragonflies, through whose translucent wings
        I see sun, stingless hornets and flat wasps—
and on occasion I cradle an ephemeral mantis
        fixed in its formidable preying stance.

None of these make it, unless I'm quick.
So who is it that I save?
Bumble bees who can swim for a limited minute.
Crickets, black and green, who walk water.
Flying ants who last an hour or even more:
        I've swooped them from the drowning waters
        and set them on the ledge to watch their
        resuscitation, as if they'd been trained—
        blowing miniscule bubbles out their mouths
        flexing their soaked diaphanous wings
        flapping them furiously until they stiffen
        and lift their resurrected bodies in flight
        to make summer another day longer than fate.

The greener-than-grass frogs hiding
in pool cracks eye this rescue with suspicion
hoping mother night will fell them manna
more than they could ever pray to eat

Grasping Grace

I'm amazed at the way you take it
as if it were a cup of sweet southern tea
served with lemon slice in ice
sipped slowly under sprawling angel oaks
        you've spoken about it so often
I'm almost used to it—
how you laugh at aging and revere
each metamorphosis precious
        the confederate jasmine clinging to our trellis
has yet to sprout a mellow bloom
but neither of us are ready to cut it down
for we know of second chances
        stumped trees line our land spouting fresh branches
jungleMagnolia, sweetGums, greeningPoplars
those tall pines have watched the foxes come and go
while I've marveled at the way your hands open and close
        you'll grasp the grace when it's handed you
for you've touched it already and already know—
while I can only guess the scents of paradise
you've taken back a petal or two

for Georgia

Experiencing Un-omniscience

Outside our windows stormclouds razored the sky,
slicing it to shreds of darkness. Lightning lashed the night
like some punitive master making all creatures rush for cover.
As the stormwinds stormed furiously and rains clobbered
everything green, I moaned, "there's gotta be a better way to nourish earth
than terror falling on our heads." While theodicies rumbled in my mind,
a call away our son was pinned under an overturned jeep—
just down the street—but we didn't hear his cry for help
(this un-omniscience has robbed my sleep). We didn't see him facing the edge
nor ease his pain as he grasped for breath. We couldn't be his savior
whom he was readying himself to see. Not did we know how
he was anguishing our anguish when we would be told his fate.
I can't believe we slept that night and didn't know till light
made morning that an unknown neighbor heard him calling.

for Peter

Hoping for a Few More Days

ever since Charlie went to spirit
you have been a light in my life
you have followed me like sunshine
but now you are near to ghost
and I am fearing the darkness—
every night before I sleep
I tell you "please don't leave me"

I watch the wave roll, form, rise,
peel down the line, cascade, and churn
into frothy white as it rushes to shore
and I think of your life—how full it has been
but now the blue-green has turned to white
and you are coming to your end—
I can't take it. I don't want you to die.

could you please hold on a few more days?
could you please, Sunny, shine your rays?

death is meant for others, not you,
at least not now—God, break through!
all creatures are inspired by your breath
it is so wrong to be snuffed out by death

before the death of Sunny (my golden retriever)

I Heard You Speak with Your Brown Eyes

you laid in pain all day and then
you got up and slowly walked
in your wasted-away frame to my bed—
(that was after we had a long talk
about seeing each other in the next life.
please wait for me—you and Charlie—)
anyway, you came to my bed and said
with your deep brown eyes you loved me
(Oh God! how I've loved you.)
we woke in the morning—you, me, Myrtle,
and drove, as always, to the beach.
you slowly climbed out of the car
and walked to the water's edge
and waded in the ocean for awhile
until you tired—then you rested and watched
me surf some small glassy waves
like you've done a thousand times.

I always know when I look to the shore
where your brown eyes will be—
you've stayed fixed on me ever since a puppy
and for this I have loved you—
there will never be another one just like you,
rare, beautiful, glorious in your day
like summer sunshine, like a glistening wave.

death is a robber who has stolen a gem,
but I know that I will see you again
and we will play in new beaches and oceans!

for my golden retriever, Sunny

Spotting a Hummingbird in a Hurricane

We hurry inland from falling floods
swollen seas birthing outrageous rush
    in fast force of wind mounting waves
climbing up the back side and tumbling
over the front in a spill of white upon white
    in seasurgeCrushAndPush of dunes and air
        erasing the horizon smearing the line
    between firm terrain and watery main.

A mile inland there's no sun than what's believed—
        as the slim trees bend shiver break
weeping willows uproot drooping
    elms unbranch and fly like pelicans
pines curve contort twist and vault
as we hear leaf-sizzle treesnap crash
        and the hurricane raining down wind.

During this assault I was startled to spot
        the hummingbird who lives in our woods
gripping a flailing untrellised magnolia branch
flapping in gusts like a lose haulyard—
and with wings whirling cyclone fast and furious
        helicoptering in the horrific hurricane attack
    long enough to sip some nectar from a cup
and then speed like wind through bending pines.

Hurricane Charlie, August 2004

Winyah Bay, South Carolina

Boating Past America's Second European Landing (1521)

Boating down the Wacammaw River that flows
   into an windswept bay I envision a time
before any European colonization had sprung—
   a time when Spanish slave raiders captured sixty natives
from the coastal tribes who thrived in Pawleys Island,
   Winyah Bay, and along the waterways where I live.
These tribes who worshiped the one Great Spirit, Wakan Tanka,
   were forced to become baptized Christians
among whom was Francisco de Chicora
   taken to be the slave of a judge in Hispaniola
then in Spain where Chicora learned the foreign tongue
   and fabricated stories of homeland wealth of splendid scope
to Martyr and Oveido, who spread the news through Europe.
   Chicora returned a few years later with Ayllon's expedition
that founded San Miguel de Gualdape, America's first colonization.
   Their fluent translator and trusted guide, he steered them
to Hobcaw in Winyah Bay, then escaped with other captive Indians.
   Fooled by Chicora's myths, the colony hoped for bonanza,
but found only a restless sea and sun-soaked savanna.

Huntington National Park, South Carolina

Admiring Ocean Old Oaks

Ocean old, they sprawl, stretch, gnarl, wear the sea,
      cling trellised to the drooping sky—
their HeavyBranches having shoved their way
          into sunshine without man or beast having seen
any exertion or maneuvering underneath.

As we stroll under them, we're amazed how they tangle
      with heaven, we marvel at the knobby canopy
that shades us, as generations before and beyond,
        and we imagine who laid under their boughs
drooling Spanish moss, catching summer breeze
with windTwisted trunks spiraling skyward
      then downward into bended crook and crawl—
so unlike the erect pines piercing into blue,
        the oaks hang with us—they linger 'round
our homes and grow on us like longtime friends,
they become our hands with so many clinging fingers
      grasping our longings for everlasting climbs—
this is their sacred glow, that they outlive us
        yet never forsake us like some unearthly soul
seeking release from earth's heavy burdens.

And so we never believe that one could come to an end,
      until our path brings us to a skeleton oak—
its tawny brown ashened, its angels turned to ghosts,
        and its fallen wings dry and brittle
snapping underfoot. Yet still it somehow stands
with no sap sucked from heavy earth; it stands
      heavy among the living. And I don't understand,
no I can't, why its roots got weary of seeking
        and its boughs of stretching—or could it be
that earth tires, letting us all go one by one?

Memories of Trees

After cloudbreak sunshower, through dancing light I walk
in wet sunshine, make quiet turnings, and pause among
memories of the trees. These who have witnessed
a thousand suns and moons are lights. I walk by them.
I share their earth and oxygen.

These nude trees are not ashamed to show living limbs
caressing their dead. They form a bent canopy to fallen rotting
logs spotted with fungus and mushrooms. Other decaying
beams bridge a brook I step. Here and there new sprigs
sprout from stumps and broken stone.

They have grown long without us and will verve till earth
and sky part. They are their own universe apart, their own
move and mover. As I step small between the angel oaks
and towering pines, I know my age is lost, but they, my host,
feed me mana much as light.

They are books, stories high, epic long, primed, ringed,
totems of red fox hunting, whitetail deer roaming,
Chicora searching the slender moment between sleep
and sound. Moth's wing soft touch, hurricane's brute bend
they've felt and are not stone.

They've spread their aquiline branches to beasts and men
and seen the human unmaking, the undying crimes, the rape
of earth beyond primal recognition. They have jeremiads
to moan, as I roam between spiraling shelves and live oaks
and smell their flesh speaking.

Pointing to sky, painting it, they are my higher. They are life.
They did not kill the Christ. They are genesis rising from chaos,
from hardness and crisis. They were spoken and are speaking.
Singing, chanting, exuding. I juice from them, muse them.
I imbibe their foliation.

Their journey is marked in talking leaves, whether gnarled or straight.

They have been all darkness. They have been all light. They are earth's sea in the wind, heaving off sadness. Rooted among them
  I grow words and throw them into hope like so many branches stretching for the tall sky.

Slim language for weighty sighs that I carry in sorry old sacks.
  The birds don't want my crumbs. They've got wings to climb trees,
while I've got songs. Long songs grasping for something pinnacle.
  And thin. Permeable are the leaves of meaning. Breathing still, the trees have so long to tell.

I bend around the gnarled stippled elms, as the splotched sun
  plops oblong behind the treeline break, and I admire the fall.
I stop to count the rings of remembrance and hear their witness
  to many suns squatting on their long thinning horizons
birthing a forestfull of stars.

North Island, South Carolina

Watching Beachcombers

bending, digging, shoveling
a weird cult of necromancers
combing here and there a crown conch,
a chambered nautilus, a mussel, a textile cone,
a triton, moret, King Helmet, and Imperial Volut—
once homes to seacreatures sucked by octopuses
dislodged by storms and surging surf
washed as refugees to elysian shores.
some make it there whole—a prize for the gatherers
most are halved, disfigured, despised.
children line their sandcastles with skeletons
of clams, oysters, scallops, and snails
(they shape old-looking windows and trellises)
while others fill their dark plastic bags
with hundreds of whelk, cowrie, and murex.
most get crushed in their luggage
but some are displayed high on mantles
next to photos of disembodied saints

Finding Meaning in Shells and Stars

crab's pokehole eyes
shrimp's thin covering and slim antennae
svelte shell rolled up in a scroll
        what do these minutiae signal?
what message am I supposed to get
from nomad shells becoming sand
and sandpipers scurrying for crabs?
        that there are more stars than pebbles
more galaxies than egrets and blue herons
more fish underwater than humans planet?
        then what is man
but a f a d i n g c o m e t, a t u m b l i n g vacant conch
making a naked spectacle of his end on the beach?

Winging to Secret Places

as this day rises over the horizon and flops into the sea
 I thrill at what I grasp (I'm so joyful it's painful)
I breathe epiphanies and catch meaning in flight—
 so many revelations happen before night

I wing to secret spaces so sweet and wild
 God lives there for a little while—
when the wind begins to sing, I hold private dawn
 when the sea surges to rhyme, I pencil the pungent sound

I store these images in my mind like bottles in my winery
 I relish each one—the color, texture, taste, and feel—
uncorking is dangerously ephemeral, pouring is sweet,
 swirling a mystery—is it wiser to treasure or better to drink?

I leave everylivingthing as it pristine is—
 its essence I do not steal; its nature I can't control
I catch moments as shadows racing from the sun
 my eyes inhale vanishing visions before nightfall

Dolphin Dawn

I walk to the ocean under the predawn moon
my shadow lengthens the closer I get to water
stars brighten the sky, and Venus hovers in the east
slowly the night turns to dawn as the sun dolphins—
stars disappear, Venus fades, and the moon thins
dark clouds laying serpentine on the horizon
contrast the glorious rising of the morning sun—
dark orange turning ruby red turning faint pink
a moveable Monet, colors running into each other—
I watch the waves risePeelPearlCascade
and a single line of pelicans surf its spindrift
I see they are sojourners. I'm a pilgrim not looking
for signs because I have already come across the divine!
I've seen the thoughts between God and men.

Ace Basin, South Carolina

Wandering

I wander on the wandering rivers:
the Ashepoo, Combahee, and Edisto
lined with cypress drooling Spanish moss
paddling a kayak to the beat of the cicadas—
as I spectate a moccasin curled in a limb
and gators mostly submerged in green waters—
their eyes as old as God and dinosaurs.
I, so modern, do not belong among any of them,
for they were here long before I encroached
but I try to be a quiet alien they might host—
I would like to transform myself into ghost
that spirits down these rivers as sunrays
and float down these rice fields as a spook
that lingers on like a poem that God once spoke.

Visiting Mempkin Monastery

on this acreage called Mempkin*
secret, serene, and lovely
the long oaks twist in every wind
seeking sun's strength.
the old monks blend, bend,
searching the ancient Almighty.
natives prayed here long before,
imbibing Wanka Tanka's Spirit.
a river runs through it
slow as ancestral memory,
strong as God, good giver of breath.

I am none of them—
oak, monk, native, river, God,
yet I feel them
breathing hard.
I'd like to climb
live inside the oaks
stretch my branches
over the river
in spirited thoughts,
a river that runs
from the mouth of God.

Mempkin means "serene"

Enjoying Earth

I am earth, not angel
the long cavernous sinew, splotched, gnarled.
I am earth, not fire,
a wandering river, restless forest, marled.
I am earth, not air
weightier than water, crumpled, restless, scarred.
I am earth, not spirit
rooted, sandblown, bent, buckled, hard.
I am earth, so much earth
I cling sky, clutch greens, waters hold.
I am earth, dead earth,
alive again, seasoned, seeded, young and old.
I am earth, not heaven hung,
raw and dust, mortal tired, bent and curled.
I am earth, slow and slumped,
blind and spent, giving and gone from.
I am earth, animaled earth
with birds, dogs, whistles and whines.
I am earth, not angel:
spirits come and moan through me as wind.
I am earth, the grave of all,
the hider of secrets, where sorrow stops.
I am earth, fecund and spermed,
seeded, sweetened, soaked, and sunned.
I am earth, blood of rivers
fountainhead of rhythm, ebb and tide.
I am earth, good God alive
with seabreeze, salt, sweat, mud and spit.
I am earth seen, songed, and sung,
spun through a multitude of rhymes.
I am earth, humaned to death,
about to get palingenesis in second breath.

Hiking Hellhole Swamp

vapid damp soil oozes over my boots
  as I trudge through swamp mud and roots
of cypresses tangled like old spider webs.
  everything smells dank, torpid, musty
in this hellhole sunken beneath sea level
  I conjure Swamp Fox and his revolutionaries
ambushing British then fleeing to this murkiness—
  maybe they were here, I imagine, as I slosh
my way forward in the plushmud—
  suddenly I see sunlight arrowing through the trees
but there's no way west or east—I'm as lost
  as the mosquitos sucking blood from my neck—
and then in the middle of this sheol
  I wander across a band of tiger swallowtails
fluttering around some secret sweetness—
  earth's angels resurrecting God's presence

Awakening The Great Circle

Wasichus' treaty said our land would be ours
    as long as grasses grow and waters flow—
you can see it's not the grass and river who've forgotten.

Our men are dark in the lostness of their eyes.
    they've dried out like parched corn, smoked tobacco ash,
strewn deer skulls. They hobble with their canes
    looking to earth for something they can't remember.

I had a dream that's wiser than waking.
    I saw the shapes of all things spirit,
the shapes of all shape as they breathe together
    in the great circle, the hoop of awakening.

I saw the face of earth's day appearing,
    where deer roam the savannahs like cloud shadow
where forests are thick as bear fur
    and where all the two-leggeds and four-leggeds
breathe the yellow air afraid of nothing.

Bull Island, South Carolina

Whirling Fury

sometimes
they can be tracked
mostly they move
their own mind
making the most
capable crazy
they don't plan attack
like reasonable men
but have a way
of taking over
when they siren
to shore
on the wheel
the round wheel
the wheel
within the wheels
the eye within
the round eye
circling unconsciously
furiously flashed
pushing the clock
backward to
heartpounding halt
as the engine
speeds by black
a sea-sucking
tongued funnel
whirling fury
on our land
through thin
structures
mostly man

Hurricane Bertha, September 1996

Broken Open Ocean

broken open ocean,
such strong faces form on you
as you leap from the abyss, peel off,
and fall all over yourself—
    that is when your waves are best

you break me with force louder than voice
of the mingled roar of wind and wave—
you suck all my strength away—
    as I swim weak into your potent wake

broken open ocean,
savage sea with warrior waves
and power longer than thought,
stronger than human mind or might,
    I break in humility, confess your majesty

your thrust forces me to my knees—
I cannot stand, I stagger in the wend,
bottomed out, I cannot blame or scold
    that I am old and you are always younger

Awendaw River, South Carolina

Watching Curves and Flow

as I watch the sun dance the river
I see that light can't be stopped
    it bends around trees
        like a corner kick
nor is water dammed
    it swerves around walls
        like a mad striker

always curves and flows

no straight line rivers any maps

    the crooked is divine
    zigs and zags
        are expected
even the long penciled stroke on the sea's horizon
is a myth

but humans
liking perfection
keep straining
        to
        go
        straight
        up
        the
        middle

Isle of Palms, South Carolina

Gazing at Night Sky

why don't you, gracious presence, stay, intensify—
more than moon grow fuller in my night's sky
        or sneak Indian summer before the brittle fall?
this invisible flow, this Spirit of your person
comes to me and surrounds me in epiphany
        as when you broke the tomb. but no show of face.
my dead body will release you and God will run
wilder than prophets' dreams. to see you as you are.
        (too hard for me, a spit of flesh, to comprehend)
yet I have nothing else to hang on—only the wind
bending trees and your Spirit hovering in mine,
        moving, sweetening dread time, loving me deeply
for no good reason, giving me grace for mistakes,
grace for aging, grace for not going yet. crazy.

Tugged by the Sea

dragging the sky behind with draught horse pull,
    it lugs me out of sleep, plants out of soil,
and stars out of hiding; lunar-powered
    it heaves heavy waters from chasm to shoal

it's no mystery I feel wrested and tugged
    toward some predestined shore,
a sled hooked to an invisibleInvincibleAnimal
that keeps pulling me relentlessly—
    I know not upward, outward, or downward

I keep groping inward thinking there's
    a hitch but since I don't ever feel I've grasped it
I grip its tethers for the ride of my life
    as I am dragged to God only knows where

Sullivan's Island, South Carolina

Scanning Beasts of Waves

on the horizon this morning
I scan beasts of waves
running from the northern coasts to the south
    like a Serengeti migration of a million wildebeests
        which, according to African legend, had to have been
            put together by a God who likes the look of clowns

on shore I see waves rushOutOfTheSea like animals
    and recall how animals c r a w l e d o u t of the sea like waves
when gills turned to lungs and flippers into paws
    and wings that flew dry skies above wet oceans—
we all had breathed oceans, we all swam seas
we are nautical, benthic, pelagic, full of sea water
    in our veins, our heart pumping waves of blood
        throughout a terrestrial body of dry bones

no wonder I yearn to abandon this island
    and rejoin my oceanic kinWithGillsAndFins

I'd like to dive head-first like a cormorant
    turning wings into flippers to swim deep oceans

Immersed in God's Ghost

phantasmic fog baptizes the island—
I'm immersed in God's ghost
the sun is covered by a swarm of clouds
    like ghostly locusts
        high in the western sky the moon appears
            then vanishes behind a veil of mist

if there was anywhere to meet God
this would be it—if I could transfigure
into spirit and go into ghost, I'd see his visage

I know we're not the same (the divine and human)
but I believe we could share the same air
if only for a little while
    like man and dolphin
        meeting on the surface of the ocean

Charleston, South Carolina

Spooked by Ghosts of Charleston

Spanish moss dangles on the oaks
in Battery Park overlooking the bay
as did an entire pirate crew—
their bodies swaying in the wind
they hung there for four long days
until they turned into ghosts
and purple lighting splashing the sky—
a supernatural emanation of their spirits
half-dead, half-living, hanging
somewhere between earth and heaven
they are drifting shadows,
eerie vibrations, headless spooks
haunting antebellum Battery Row

they appear as thin apparitions—
visitors hear their faint footsteps,
watch doorknobs turning, doors opening
and feel a RushOf Ghost pass by—
they mingle with others long gone
Confederate soldiers who lost the war
and their bodies in fierce battle
they roam Charleston's gated streets
they stride the red brick roads
unwilling to migrate to the next life—
they hang on live oaks like moss
as spooks and sprites suspended—
their life on earth has never ended

Folly Beach, South Carolina

Witnessing the Miracle of Ocean

a strong northwest blows in
turning the beach into a desert sandstorm
strong enough to knock me off my feet—
      the ocean is wild with waves
I have yet to brave
for now, I watch the miracle of ocean
waves churning forward breaking into foam
      glassy walls rising and falling
colliding with waves that fell before them—
the moving sea is wonderful for imagination
      I don't tire of watching its undulations –

above the night sky rolls
with millions of stars, night suns like ours,
and exploding supernovae becoming black holes
whorling, whirlpooling vortexes—
      destruction and creation without end

Musing under a Starlit Ocean

when all is darkened on the island
I look at starlit skies and muse about deities
    who once thickened the swirling cosmos—
mixed myriads populating the invisible
evil spirits mingled with good
    shadows bright with jinn and shen
spiriting everywhere nowhere known
daimonia, deities, pleroma, angels
    gods who created then took off
with other names to other kingdoms
while I am left to figure chaos

that's why prophets came, they said
Zarathustra spake "the gods are dead"
    only Ahura Mazda is LordAllWise
author of evil, maker of good
sainted Satan, ambivalent God.
    Moses proclaimed the IAMwhoIAM
YaHWeH EverExistingOne.
others abandoned the heavens
    (strange to the spot were in)
Mahavira beat his karma to death
attaining moksha, sweet release.
    Siddhartha saw flesh, couldn't starve
desire, craved truth, drank nirvana.
Lao-tzu found Tao, the sacred flow
    while wise Confucius said nothing new

these all discovered life and death themselves
then Another came, not to explain
    demons, devotions, pangs and trouble
but to face the human loathe with love,
not to raise apothegm from the crypt
    but to create. This was healer of longsick
curer of sin-death, paintaker, paradiser,
pioneer of the tenebrous curse
    who said he was himself the way
        then journeyed beyond the grave

Night Ocean

I take off like an unchained star
      in private peregrinations
(some obscure some dim some unlit)
not part of any constellation—
the journey of thought is too quick to collect
too heavy to weigh, too black to paint—
      under the sun it was once different
when I saw pelicans dip and dive in ocean wind
these were dimensions I could maneuver
I could even find my way around faces
      and read them like maps
but everything in darkness changes shape

so I wait for a slim streak of light
      to turn my black to gray and gray to white
but nothing is going to change until dawn—
the blackness had done this, the murkiness
at one time, I remember, the sea was lucid
the bottom was clear enough to see the trout
      swim between the reef and rocks
but now the sky is mud
bending shadows, breaking myths

Sensing the Spirit of the Sea

       Earth rises to meet this morning's glow,
Spirit souls the sea, breathes into waves, windclimbs,
       billows, heaves brutebends, buckle, gnarl, cave,
while beachcombers trimBrimBendCurlHurl
       in the wave of, crest of, flung fetch of welter,
whether borreal, austral, euroclydion, or western—
       the four winds of zoatic pneuma verve, gush
zephyrs, sproutBulbous, spillUnctuous, cleave
       reefs, island man, smashing cliffs, rock
and those who mean to surf the meanest break.
       Most have to take the gentler smoother roll,
the sweeter stuff of waves, the lighter
       and smaller peels, not breaking them to coral

Thinking of Lost Friends

the sun never rose today
    at least that I could see
I watch the waves roll in the sea
    and recall friends who used to be

they were like fluted sounds breathed out
    into distant seagreen hollers—
the souls I thought I knew passed
    while the tune we sang lingers

unladened unmanned ships sent out
    into wild darkgreen rollers—
the spirits I tried to know go
    while the course I hold wanders

smoke rising from snuffed candles
    into the swirled blueblack yonder—
the saints I knew I loved left
    while they pilgrim what I ponder

Amazed by Wind and Moon

eastwaking
it resurrects waves
ghosts fetches
presences God in eardrop silence
falls festooned, spirit rises,
numbs bones, cools downcast faces—
allpotent earthdominant wind

it blew all day under a sunny dome
until dusk calmed it down and darkness ruled

then, rising fullbodied in the east
triumphing earth, dragging ocean
in its wake, pulling heavy tidewaters
to build, brim, break, crest
with piles of water everywhere
flocks of it, swarms, seagulling,
hovering, settling, squatting—
comes the effulgent nightdominant moon

Watching Waves and Considering Eternity

when I came here as spirit from Spirit,
a wave pushed from sea, I didn't know I was
once immortal channeled into mortality

I must have liked it where I was before,
roaming with spirited angels. undying. free.
but God must think divinity is lost without faces
in whom to live and breathe his being

could it be that my life is his because it really is—
that as I am not apart from him, so he without me?

it's the mortal parting I don't get—that I will disappear
as my spirit unfleshes and wriggles out
from this tired space and crowded bones

I'll slit an opening in eternity
and slide in before anyone sees
I am there as I have always been—
waiting only for my body to give me up. quick.

Alone with the Silver Sea

silver sky smears into silver sea
       hardly a horizon to see
silver pelicans line the beach
       waiting for silver fish
to swim in the inward tide

the only white is waves' break
       c u r l i n g d o w n t h e l i n e

I am alone with the ocean
       spinning alone in the universe
trying to find an ancient God or modern self—

when I stride close to the pelicans
       they fly into the smoothsilverSky
above the silver sea
       and they wind-surf the break
running down the argent line
       and when they land, my dogs chase them
into the sunlit moving ocean

Stiff-legging into October Surf

As I stiff-leg a sandy trail from marsh to ocean
    I hear what the waves appear to be
and can't wait to immerse my head in water
        warmer than the air. I'll push my legs to bend
one more session as I come to where sea lands
        and moves a man still strong enough to paddle
and aged enough to know I won't always
        have strength to break beyond the breaking surge.

But for this day I am good enough, as I am drawn
        by the cresting and curling sea exploding
into whiteness from dark nothing. I'm awed by swells
        mounting to shore with epiphanic faces.
It's amazing that the rude ocean lines up in the end:
        beachcomber after beachcomber rakes
shoals, beach, and brim in even strokes.

And all this because a hurricane churns the Atlantic our way,
        pushing northeastern waves for days on days—
in sweet swells pearling to the surfer's left
        blowing spindrifts in occasional offshore gusts,
or in strong rushes shoaling too swiftly to catch.

The day before the hurricane hits, I surf to the end
        of my strength, until the last glory of dusk,
as the clouds overhead clutch as much sheen as they can
        in an eerie glimmer brightening before it dims.

In the morning the outer bands circle our way,
        dropping sky into sea, pummeling ocean into sand;
by afternoon the typhoon has swallowed sun
        and risen leviathan in ocean lunging at land,
pounding the pier, crushing a few crazed surfers—

it's wild, it's weird, it's the wind conquering earth
whenever it can. And it does it best with heaps of water
        so beastly beautiful, so awfully powerful,
so close to killing and kind to quicken liquid into breakers.

Kiawah Island, South Carolina

Walking under the Long Sun

strong clouds rise this morning
drastic lightning that spooks darkness
        heavy surge that cannot be tamed
palms bending in the wind coloring heaven
and then the long sun comes
        putting distance into time

the oblong sun turns into a slow moon

and then an epiphany of stars signs
our insignificance. each evening it happens:
the sky falls off and dogs into haze
(another page ripped off the book)

I prefer the unloneliness of day
one sun in the sky. light and easiness.
        night is for sleeping. not looking up
where wings and lost thoughts ghost
the dark griffin-like, where ancient mariners
        in caravans cruise celestial spheres
searching for other Jerusalems, I guess

against unmastered dark,
clouds spirit past paper flimsy
        thinner than sky, thinner than skin
translucent with moonshine
bursts and flashes of it
        as fatter spirits bloat and bleed
move as wind into wind
between us and the uncut beyond
        the facelessness of space
lost in stars, masses of nameless stars
birthing and dying, bright then black

in moving wind clouds transfigure and figure.
and I imagine meaning breaking through

and going long in the long march of clouds,
the souls of God, fleeting creatures
seeking light to break their glory on

Enjoying Sunlight on the Beach

I like beach sunlight. shafts of it. casting shades
        and shadows long and bare. openness between trees.
leaves sucking air. illuminated sand.
        I was always edgy with cities lit up with headlights
weaving through murkiness and lamplights
        laboring to heave off heavy darkness.
it cannot be shoveled away
        as if it were snow or sand. only dawn exorcises.
ah brightness! handfuls. bucketfulls. barrelfulls.

I cannot imagine more lucid glory
        than what surrounds. clouds mingle with sun,
light with wind s t r e t c h i n g greens into glistening shades
        and blue is so pleasant to the sky.
I am spirited with these lights, these lives.

        what red is thicker than the woodpecker's hood—
what flash of orange than oriole's wing?
        no gold is purer than the snowy egret's iris.

so fluid, fair, unpretentious, stems of light
        shoot through leaves in peregrine plunge,
falconSpiral, seahawkDive, heronBob.
        light arches, curves, and heaves heaven.

light is sweet. stems of it. blazed. uncolored
        undying, unstruggling, not having to breathe.
it's wind I've never seen bending around long objections
        it travels seas, traverses minds, and always returns
pure, untired. untainted, its aura inheres, inspires.
        never the-dark-no-exit. but the unexpected exodus—
the journey so sweet, so gracious, so for the making.

the light is face, God's face. God's mouth. coming out.

when light leaves the eyes like an old man
        trying to get out his house for the last time

on cane on crutches on anything but help
     on longings for winterless woods
where streams of sunshine green everylivingthing—
     when this light creeps out from behind the eyes
the spirit goes with it slowly, at first, like a cat
     testing the ground with its front paws,
like a dog sniffing the wind for wild scent,
     but then it knows it's right to wend, to leap
not into the grim unknown but to its own
     sacred air and breath and break of glory
I've seen the light fade in faces only to return
     for one brilliant blast as when a cloudcast day
turns gloriously sudden at sunset's end.
     Some have patina. others luster. aureole is so hard
     to grasp. luminosity harder to sustain.

Walking the Shore and Wondering Where All the Souls Go

day passes into dusk and dusk to night
when stars lighting darkness come out
as I gaze into the evening sky I'm amazed
      that there are universes apart from this
stuffed with plethoric visibleness
and angels, zillions of them, thin as light
      and spirits ghosting between the galaxies

but where do all the souls go
those murdered for good
those who killed sorrows
and those who leaped light—
      do they wander to some nova birthing stars?

somewhere between intangible and thrust
there is no waiting for the ship to come
      no imagining but becoming the imagined
somewhere between the cracks of dawn
and dusk I rush back into the mouth of God
      and come out singing there is sense

Crooking the Straight

the morning oval sun coming into dawn
tells me today is a day for curves and rounds
I unhorizontal the fixed
crook the straight, bend it into bows
like curling waves, eyeballs
and egg-shaped sun on the horizon
I round every even thing
I warp the long straight rod
defunct the period
snap the bracket, make ellipsis, kill end rhyme
time is not my murderer anymore
ovoid God

I coil spin twist even if I tangle it is superior
the arc of arch, the bow of bend, never the end
of hollowing the hallowed
all is rolled
as I vault the void and sphere into near by far

ragged is the rolling moon tonight
the edge, the dropoff
into whatever that is—the linear lies
the circular the round the bend is unchartered
I frontier thee on unsmooth edge
by faith against an end

/

Admiring a Moving Tapestry

waves of flocks color the sea's horizon
as seagulls, pelicans, cormorants, terns,
(each with their own brilliant kind)
weave in and out of each other
making a moving tapestry as divine
as anything angelic we could witness
on earth—they are like sacred spirits
ghosting the air, hosting heaven's
gift to our world; a swarming miracle,
dropping like manna, ascending on high,
they quickly rise, swiftly fall like waves—
an aerial ocean above the heaving seas.

I have often prayed to be bird
not belonging to anyone but God,
to wing in flocks, soar surging seas,
to be as close to wind as spirit
is to angels, to rise and fall free.
how I'd love to have hollow bones,
soft feathers, and clutching talons,
to swoop into the aqua ocean
and snatch a speeding mackerel—
if there could be a samsara miracle,
I'd moksha now and spirit myself
into that pelican surfing wave's face!

Seabrook Island, South Carolina

Imagining Zoa in the Night Sky

the night sky over the ocean is so clear
    I see zodiacal signs and I imagine
the living Zoa Ezekiel and John
    saw around the Almighty's throne—

the Zoa have been the mind
    of the moving Maker
living in being, spirits of the Spirit,
    zoapoetic in shape, flash,
metaform, flowing, and glow—
    they are emanations of procreations,
God's glance and gaze, divine sweep,
    flutter, soar, and sail
        they rapture me into more and making

they are the thoughts
    between now gone and next
the imaginations of children
    before they're etched
flowing into clouds like angels,
    ephemeral, wet—
they swarm the skies
    like so many clouds in swirl
they swash my sight
    like flamingos lifting in flight
clearer than gods and more serene,
    they move as lights
as they aspire from here
    to there migrating desires
they circle by wing of soul,
    by thrust of gentleness
in sun stroke, moon pull,
    togetherness and glide
they take my thoughts
    and brave them into otherness

by vault, spring of being,
        swift skip into muse and making—
the pounce after pondering,
        the catch of contemplation—
they are the fetch of imagination,
        the wing of flight, the sight of seeing,
the long strong pulse of sacredness,
        the apotheosis of promised
hopes and inspirations
        their wings sing them from wind
to flung far—the stretch of, the slim leap,
        the long faith and reach into elation
without pause or ponder
        they are afloat, numinous lumens,
multiple faces, places I've never been,
        songs I've not yet tuned
they seep, smile, send
        me into longing for words—
they thin the membrane
        between now and ever
as I unflesh into float, fling,
        free, rise and slide almighty,
                sieving soul through permeable heaven

Watching Migrations in Early October

it's early October in Carolina
when creatures metaphysic south
most in broods and pools:
pelicans, cormorants, egrets
arrowing blue heavens

spots, whitings, blues
chased by black cold and sharks.
my instincts tell me follow
but there's no way to morph
unless I quickly wing or fin

somehow chrysalis uncocoons
from pupa darkness with wings
colored sunrise and surprise:
there is transfiguration—
God can change after all

leaving behind shed
blood and skin these miracles
fling into translucent cherubim—
metamorphosis in flight
gives us rise to sing!

as I worm along the beach
one by one they flit pass
magnificent every few minutes
following the coast religiously
on some appointed route

I gaze at their salmon wings
painted with black auspice
praying to divine the sign
as each alone pilgrims
to a home it's never been

Feeling the End of Summer

summer is nearly over
I hear the weather falling
fear the failing sun
they're gone like souls
disappeared and sainted

but I remember a few weeks
ago watching their noiseless wings
move them quicker than waves
and I'm braved to imagine a place
even God would like to live

if they know where to fly
at summer's end shouldn't I
sense when paradise begins
and lift imago wings
to austral winds and rise?

yes! when the call comes
to uncocoon and unfurl
diaphanous wings thin as angels
flying nowhere near imagination
I will split, flare, and wend

Viewing Flocks of Monarchs

flocks of monarchs flit pass, seeking southern sun—
      how I thirst to become light and wing with them
out of sight of winter's too old, too cold eyes—
      my mind unscrolls with these voyaging cherubim
to warm Mexican mountains, to Pacific groves.

how I'd love to journey with these angelic gypsies
      who beat death by beating silent wings.
I read their flight in volumes of message—
      each monarch a floating book, thin as papyrus
written in black ink with story older than Scripture,
      bolder than Moses shouting from the bush.

I have somewhere to follow better than sadness
      when I worm out of this body, turn chrysalis,
shed blood and skin, unravel wings to the winds,
      free fly, free rise, unweighted, unabated
into more soar than transfigured dream

I am going where I've never been or seen
      to a joyous panegyric I taste with my spirit.
I will join the million myriads gathered in the air
      suspended between this earth and heaven
in flocks of festal orange enjoying journey's end—
      with the best of transmigration yet to begin.

we will come again to grace woods and meadows
      to wing and whirl. our leaving means parousia is near—
as it is written on our paper pinions, we are circular
      minions: death to us is life and life is not death,
as we give voice without ever making noise.

Admiring Wings

while I put wings on flat words and fly them
   across sheets and sheets of thin paper,
      every October they migrate farther than thought:
         red ladybugs, death's head hawkmoths,
            painted lady butterflies, libellula dragonflies,
         and the glorious monarch butterflies
      whose wings fling them to Mexican mountains
   where they congregate with a million pilgrims,
making me believe there's solid heaven beyond every verb

as I sense their presence come, the presence goes,
   an invisible feel I've come to know—
      a finger of cool wind turns my head
         to spot a monarch undulating near the sea,
            light a rose, sip nectar, unceremoniously ascend—
         though I know her invisible eyes don't glory
      in the beauty of her magical majesty,
   I wonder if she's aware, as she flings wings south
she's been marked to be my pioneer

Watching Wings Thin as Wind

northborntransformed
    chrysalis makes solo farflight
living on God, on angels,
    on wings as thin as wind
with thinner mind it pilgrims
    above myriad meadows
mountains seacoasts and men
    to its panegyric heaven
in festive flocks of orange—
    transcendent monarchal worm

Breathing

emerged from the silver sea
    a hump of bestial beauty
levitating a moment between
    aquatic and aerotic worlds
then with brimming face pudgy and serene
    pushed a glow into everywhere dark—
before taking a quick breath of light
    and plunging into invisible silver.

though the rest of the day was gray
    I breathed lighter
thinking how close I got to God.

Seeing Sprouting Wings

a butterfly fluttered in the tall wind
sprouting monarchial wings
thin as angels but substantial—
the corporeal color of heaven u n f u r l i n g,
as it floated between the longleafed boxtrees
through cedars, oaks, and cypress
moving majestically easy—

transfigured, fair, and nature's master—
flitting wings papyrus sheer
transparent, bloodred, untorn
unaware of its sway.
In quick season it would pilgrim
the bends and ascend its way
to the gathering of myriads more

Walking under Sun

the sun breaks brilliantly.
as I walk, my shadow stretches far to the west
as the sun rises higher
my shadow gets shorter
by noon it is one in the same,
body and spirit sharing one form—
they will split apart
when body changes to spirit

I know we humans are spirit, elohim,
inferior only to cherubim.
with elongated wingspans we stretch edges
and think we can fly an unwalled sky
in all directions we imagine
but you, God, are DepthBreadthLengthHeight
your reach is incredible SOMUCHSO
that we cannot fill our spirits with you
just as we can't swallow any star we see—
oh, you put us at such a grave distance
when you breathed us into flesh
(o u r m i n d s f l a s h w a y b e y o n d o u r g r a s p)
we hate that earth encloses our bones
but we refuse to entomb, we rescind to ash.
I call on you great God to act:
rip off the broken pinions, slit the tethers!
imp my crimped wings with divine feathers!

Coasting

before dawn a sliver of moon hangs in the sky
long clouds line the horizon soon transformed
     by sunshine from gray beasts into flaming dragons
mouths open wide to swallow the orb as it rises
but aurora breaks through conquering the monsters with light—
     glory wins the day as the sky succumbs to brilliant rays

pelicans coast along the waves—wind surfing—
hardly needing to flap their wings as they undulate
     in the drafts of wind just in front of the breaks
my dogs speed down the beach chasing seagulls
who rise as one then scatter into the heavens
     then descend one by one to bob on the ocean

as always, outside is fresh and blood for me
the ocean breaks open bread, light in me opens
the sky pours wine, God falls to my tongue
     I taste divinity dropped and start to hum

Stream around Seabrook Island, South Carolina

If I Were Spirit

I just missed the hissing bobcat bounding in the bush
and a siting of puma roused me
          to search on the morrow he didn't appear.
the marsh hummed as always with cicada strum
                    the stream sung as ever over fallen rock
if I were spirit everywhere I could watch.

other signs are fixed as sun moon stars
their constancy carries the flight of day
          and beaches boundaries for my swelling thoughts.
wave after wave connects the drifting continents
          where natives spot the cheetah slinking past the dark
and fishers catch the meaning of a broken net.

Edisto Island, South Carolina

Enjoying the Rhythm of the Ocean

an orange swath lays on the horizon
just before the sun dawns
      then the oval egg emerges from the ocean
         mother of regeneration

pelicans fly across her path
dolphins porpoise in the waves
blue herons begin to fish
and my dogs chase rays
trapped in tide pools
near the symphonic ocean—

one wave after another percussing
      the sizzle droning
         the wind blowing through it like a flute

all is alive with spirit-life
      breathing the dawning sun
         my spirit jumps and I dance
            to the rhythm of the sea

Watching the Ocean Spill

over and over the ocean spills
dark ink on paper
over and over the sea speaks poetry
and the poet finds rhyme
   in God who is Spirit of the sea

as living scripture
a wave of wind passes
peaking in perfection
pearling in otherness, nowness—
   the realness of Godness

light escapes darkness for a rhyme
light in the living sea oracles mightily
over the waves it pulsates
under the wave it lumens
   and it will always shine

there is light everyway
you want to see
in the excellence of presence
the pure clear radiant host
   mingled with invisible awe

Combahee River, South Carolina

Finding Freedom in 1863

while the ink was wet on the proclamation of emancipation
Tubman guided 150 black Yankee soldiers down the Combahee
(the river I am now passing under dripping hot sun)
they floated in gunboats destined to set the slaves free
who ran out of the woods from behind these cypress trees
with hands raised in the air and shouts of glorious liberty—
800 of them climbed into the boats and heard Harriet sing:

"Of all the whole creation in the East or in the West
The glorious Yankee nation is the greatest and the best!
Come along! Come along! Don't be alarmed.
Uncle Sam is rich enough to give you all a farm!"

at the end of the verse they lifted their hands and shouted "glory!"
freedom from tyranny had unchained them that very day—
unshackled from the dreaded curse of God-awful slavery
they traveled to Beaufort, then north, freed from the Confederacy

Caught Up in the Catch

I watch the men casting their nets, fling after fling,
  and recall a time when the natives used to fish here:
the young men muscled their way against the breakers
    six in each dugout canoe stroked in unison and sang
until about 100 yards out they stopped and dropped
    a 100 foot-wide dragnet, spreading the seine in the shining sea,
then paddled back to shore with the two end lines—
    while two swimmers stayed out to keep the net taut
the other 10 divided themselves between the two lines
    and began a long arduous pull of net to shore.
as they pulled on the long ropes, they chanted and sang:
    "give us fish, o Lord," *huh-huh*; "give us fish, today" *huh-huh*
"give us fish, o Lord" *pull-pull*; "give us fish today" *pull-pull.*
    older villagers wrapped the lines around bending palms
that wore the grooves of a thousand previous catches
    as they watched the young men cross the lines in an X
to trap the fish they'd been dragging toward the beach
    as the silver fish began flashingAndpoppingUpWildly,
the seabirds hovering on tottering wings just above them,
    women appeared with baskets balanced on their heads,
children romped with glee in the foaming shallows
    and were allowed to join in the beautiful pull
with the native villagers caught up in the catch!

Contemplating the Wild

what does it matter that I've lived and died
        in a cosmos gone completely wild
killing stars, birthing stars,
        creating aeons of new planets
the visible erupting from the invisible
        billions of stars fleshing into fullness—
new galaxies on the outermost reach
        of an expanding, unfolding universe—
Creator divines the universes into being
        the wild Word oracles billions of galaxies—
our Milky Way stars in the evening sphere
        the moon kingdoms deep dark nights
the golden orb spirits oceans and fecund earth
        where fish porpoise seas, birds sun in trees
giraffing into the bright blue cylinder sky
        and wild animals forest deep dark woods
snaking, monkeying, squirreling, loping—
        no-footeds, two-footeds, four-footeds
roaming trillions of verdant rolling acres
        buffaloing the mind's ability to grasp
how many earth-like planets in this cosmos
        are the precious objects of God's lionization

Blufton, South Carolina

Watching Duck Hunters

camouflaged clothes, camouflaged boats
    shotguns loaded, duck decoys in hand
        excited retrievers, noses sniffing the dark air
            above the Savannah River before early dawn
        they launch into the winter mist hanging there—
and it's not too long till I hear the gun blasts
and imagine ducks falling off the edge of the sky

Viewing Savannah Cattails

the head heavies to neck bending
and uglies, turning autumn ash—
don't despise those unsightly facial hairs—
they're but semeia of transfiguration:
>   *my soul is unburdening, puffing bright,*
splitting into a million seeded tufts
waiting to catch wind—once blown apart
>   *I'll be scattered, sown, and grown for good*

>   *just try to drown me—my corky drift fruit*
will fare the sea and loft in Atlantic flotsam.
>   *or burn me to the ground—I'll crack open*
bright fireweed seed in a whirling cloud
smart colors unfurl, unveiled designs astound—
the seed is revelation that life wills life on

Admiring Wildlife

an archipelago of low islands
receiving waves of the Atlantic ocean
lines the southern South Carolina coast—
human presence has virtually vanished,
its history haunted by moaning ghosts
of slaves chanting in the rice plantations,
their songs mingling with winds rattling palmettos
growing here and there in the salty marshlands
spotted with cord grass, cattails, and bulrushes.

the tidal creeks teem with fish and fowl:
wandering whimbrels, godwits, oyster catchers,
redknots, dunlins, willets, and plovers—
thousands of birds unperturbed by humans
fly free and fish hungrily on mullets and minnows
who are also a feast for wood storks, egrets
ibis, pelicans, whooping cranes, and bald eagles.

the marine-green maritime forests roll on and on
like waves and waves of the Atlantic ocean—
these woods, home to foxes, bobcats, jaguars,
meander all the way down the Carolina coast.
I'd love to wind along the creeks and rivers
that meander through the live oaks and cypresses
and listen to nothing else but their voices.

Hilton Head Island, South Carolina

Sighting a UFO

the four of us beachwalkers
were keeping the sea and stars to ourselves
as we listened to waves percussing on shore
talking of the day and nothing more
when suddenly there was an epiphany—
       a flood of light crashed on our faces.
it was not moonlight or starlight
but an extraterrestrial beam from above—
we all looked up—jaws dropping, eyes popping
as we gazed at a saucer flying and spinning
above our heads, silently hovering—
       transfixed by this otherworldly appearing
none of us said anything
until after the spacecraft ascended in a second
out of sight into the dark heavens

Admiring the Sea-scapist

Spirit, sea-scapist, spreads blue on sky's canvas
paints clouds with bright sunlight
colors waves porpoising on the littoral
draws variegated shades of green
with white froth foaming on the brims—
some are painted in the act of forming,
others as they rise, pearl, and break—
   all are miracles of power and grace,
each wave's face revealing a Creator—
the ever-moving, ever-living,
zoatic, pneumatic, aquatic artist
   never letting his paint dry, as the creation
waves and flows like a fluid van Gogh:
seabirds fly across the moving canvas
dogs run along the changing seacoast
dolphins leap, breaking the rolling surface—
   all is alive with living God
who lives, moves, and has his being
in all the creatures he keeps painting—
he is the flow that makes the ocean
he is the blue that makes the sky
he is the water that makes the rain—
   the painter himself is the living paint

Witnessing an Epiphany of Wind on Sea

the aurora angels through the clouds
divinity breaks upon creation once again—
an epiphany of wind on sea and sun

I crave light even though it makes me thirst
a world full of light and water is better
than either by themselves

I will walk the sea and study water
they are my Rabbi and Buddha master

the waves have no reason to be but for beauty
each lives and dies quicker than a mayfly
and yet they keep coming like stallions
on the run, a never-ending herd—
their white manes flowing in the wind
their gallant bodies rushing break-neck to shore—

there are always more and more and more
each living and dying in successive generations
yet always sustaining the moving sea—

my life is a wave

Marveling at the Wave

inscrutable abysmal
  your genesis is darkness
    lost in shapelessness, void
      an obscure voice speaks you
        pushes you to pilgrimage
          there is no will to stop
            as you undulate cap froth
            and you are hurricane driven
            by storms by fetch by sound
            passed vessels safe and sunk
            you are the Maker in motion
            the globe's visible undulation
            the breathing of the sea
          our planet's potency and pull

I am drawn to the coast
  to watch your glory mount
    from some invisible thrust
      with perfect curve and verve
        you then bowbend and kneedrop
          with brightness tumbling overhead
            as you flop in your conking roar
            (your own applause and praise)
            as another martyr dropping behind
            is just as quickly glorified and razed
            so pacific are these separate deaths
            these revelations of soul
          that I kneel at dawn's seabreak
        and pray this is how I go

Burke's Beach, Hilton Head, South Carolina

Sliding and Gliding

sunny skies. offshore wind. storm kicking waves
      a hundred miles out. blessed surf—sublimely shaped

breaking right and left in a serene northwest.
      at first I have them to myself. then others come,

I count them friends. so I don't mind sharing surge,
      s l i d e g l i d e s p l u r g e. the wave jumping high,

tubing, peeling down the line, as I ride long lefts
      to the groin. and rights all the wave back again.

others do the same as I paddle back out. some hoot.
      some holler. mostly the ocean sings. it soothes,

it moves, as spirit sustains. windandSeaandSun
      and man in confluence: evidence that God is good.

Eating Sunlight

earlier the night was between us
now I'm alone in the sun's wind
          that blows though royal palms
whose leaves hymn the Almighty
as they rustle and drone like waves
that take the shapes of spirits
          that come and go, as the sea crests
in blue, lapis lazuli, turquois, and white—
what a sight: ocean waving
like wind-blown fields of wheat

I want to sit here and eat sunlight
like the moia of Easter Island
I am still. I am here. Still here.

I can swim through darkness
          in the quiet divine presence
                    who doesn't need to say to speak

Watching God Disappear

sometimes God disappears
behind some royal palm tangled in the light
the wind taking him away like brilliant thoughts

I watch clouds fluff, flag as they're eaten by sky
and wonder what I'd do if he rained on me
since I've come to believe in the invisible

the stallion waves come rushing to shore
then disappear just as quickly in the surf
earth is a good forever place I believe

Stepping out of Water

I step out of water and ocean falls off. I am mammal. land.
earth. defrocked and naked, I seek hermitage in recluse waves

and look long for overcast oceans to break fast
and take me. Down. Under. Away. Out. Back. In. To.

But here again I sit and contemplate my marlness
as I watch waves mount and mush, and wonder what's

our difference. As seafog sponges the coast like mist
over lovelost eyes, thinness between water and land fade.

I move, as it were, before the Spirit hovering
somewhere between wet and wildness, hesitating to utter,

to blurt, "Let the land appear dry." better it stay water.
the long surge of sea. the stretch over nothing but fetches.

water moving into waterness. dark hunkering under
darkness. No one there to call it hostile to the light.

nothing mammaling. swimming. sucking air. let not
the divide slice. better it be fog than forlorn. and rare.

Scanning the Unscrolling Sea

Its own creation, unscrolled and scrolling, a bodiless soul
taking shapes of waves, transfigured into cresting forms,

flashed into flesh it appears, then disappears in froth,
foam, blown into nothing by the spirits of zephyrs.

Sea and breeze, kindred ghosts, moisten imagination,
kick waves, wonder. Slip between thoughts and under—

they are Miraclemaking. Nothing from them can be taken.
I am immersed again. Again I seek ablution, transfiguration.

To be rid of furtive flesh. To squirm from this body just once
and become the wave I surf, the wind I breathe. Free from mortal me.

A wave gone bodiless. Wind gone everywhere
into water—to crest, peel, crash, mush, splash, foam.

Seeing Unveiled Mystery

Nothing is more beautiful than the wave, coming from God,
going back to spirit; it's manifest in so sleek a time and rhythm,

leaving the horizon it swells its own shape and rhymes its line
as it moves serenely. Music. Magic. Mystery of here and gone.

a song of shape and unshaping. the deep smooth mound of
blue blooms, forms, curls, peels, plumes brighter than cloud,

surges down the long line of sound, sagaciousness, and fury falling
into festive froth and riot of splurge surging fast and free,

like bee diving into moving aqua pistil, drinking nectar,
slide into you and out, higher than air, happier than suck.

nothing is more juicy than being in the wave. Going with God,
slipping into spirit. getting wet in so sleek a rise of rhyme.

Thinning into Wind

      I have not seen angel. Felt one, yes. Nor Jesus in flesh.
His Spirit roams earth, wet wanderer giving living water.

      Until his face I see, I hear wild wetness of his word
stirring wind and waves. He sustains. Creating creation

      as the sun swells yet again over our imagined horizon.
Never in the solidness of my flesh have I crossed

      that line to find the plume thin into wind and sea.
But spirits come to me from yonder. Slim explorers

      of the afterwave and now. They have seen more miracles
than fish. They penetrate the membrane between here and then.

      Their spirit calls the ocean out of me. And I have returned
to sea. The voice so clear, as when I first heard the waves

      breaking and God's presence as my own breathing.
I come, Lord, frontiering the ever of everlasting.

Philip Comfort has a doctorate in literary interpretation from the University of South Africa. He has been senior editor at Tyndale House Publishers for 33 years. He has taught English, New Testament, Religion, and Greek at several colleges—most recently Coastal Carolina University. He has authored over 15 academic books and five books of poetry. He lives in Pawleys Island, South Carolina, with his beloved wife Georgia.